The Wisdom of Swami Sri Yukteshwarji - Vol.1

Swami Sri Yukteshwar Giri

FOREWORD

This Book is the true Philosophy of Religion. It was compiled by my Spiritual Preceptor Sadhu - Sabhapati Swami Jiu Maharaj, to establish the truth that there is an essential unity in the basis of all religion, and published part by part in "Sadhusambad" the Journal of Sadhusabha, We usually find Christian Missionaries of the different societies preaching the religion of the Holy Bible in different sectarian forms, although the teachings of the Bible itself are quite far from that and perfectly non-sectarian.

To show that the Holy Bible wholly teaches pure Sanatan Dharma the Eternal Religion of the Indian Sadhus, I have collected these parts and publish it in book form; so that the religious public may not be misguided by the mistaken ideas of sectarianism which, we think, is the curse of Religion in its true sense.

The sanskrit sutras of this Book, having reconciled all the different technical terms used by different schools of Indian philosophy, will be also a great help in the study of 'Bhagbat Gita' the highest book in philosophy and Theology in the present world.

Atul Chandra Chowdhary,

Secretary, Sadhusabha
A.D.1920
(Dwapar 221)

Introduction

This book was written by Sri Yukteswar Giri at the request of Mahavatar Babaji in 1894.

The Fact is that the present age is Dwapar Yuga and 194 years of the Era is passed away, which is the Cause of the rapid development in all departments of knowledge. Dwapar Yuga, scientific theories were gradually reduced to practice, and they begun to contribute much to the happiness of mankind.

The Holy Science is a book of theology written by Swami Sri Yukteswar Giri in 1894. The text provides a close comparison of parts of the Christian Bible to the Hindu Upanishads, meant "to show as clearly as possible that there is an essential unity in all religions...and that there is but one Goal admitted by all scriptures."

Swami Sri Yukteswar Giri was born Priya Nath Karar in 1855 to a wealthy family. As a young man, he was a brilliant student of math and science, astrology and astronomy. He joined a Christian missionary school where he studied the Bible and later spent two years in medical school.

After completing his formal education, Priya Nath married and had a daughter. But he continued his intellectual and spiritual pursuits, depending on the income from his property to support himself and his family.

After the death of his wife, he entered the monastic Swami order and became Sri Yukteswar Giri, before becoming a disciple of famed guru Lahiri Mahasaya, known for his revitalization of Kriya Yoga.

Then in 1894, Sri Yukteswar Giri met Mahavatar Babaji, an ageless wise man who is said to have lived for untold hundreds of years. At this meeting, Mahavatar Babaji gave Sri Yukteswar the title of Swami, and asked him to write this book comparing Hindu scriptures and the Christian Bible. Swami Sri Yukteswar obeyed.

He also founded two ashrams, including one in his ancestral home. He lived simply as a swami and yogi, devoted to disciplining his body and mind, and thus to liberating his soul. Among his disciples was Paramahansa Yogananda, credited with bringing yoga and meditation to millions of Westerners.

The Holy Science consists of four chapters. The first is titled "The Gospel," and is intended to "establish the fundamental truth of creation." Next is "The Goal," which discusses the three things all creatures are seeking: "Existence, Consciousness, and Bliss."

Chapter three, "The Procedure," is the most practical of the sections. It describes the natural way to live for purity and health of body and mind. The final chapter is called "The Revelation," and discusses the end of the path for those who are near the "three ideals of life."

Swami Sri Yukteswar also displays his impressive knowledge and understanding of astrology by proposing his theory of the Yuga Cycle.

Each yuga is an age of the world that tracks the movement of the sun, Earth, and planets. Each age represents a different state of humanity.

There are four yugas:

- **Satya Yuga** is the highest and most enlightened age of truth and perfection.

- **Treta Yuga** is the age of thought and is more spiritually advanced than Dwapara Yuga and Kali Yuga.

- **Dwapara Yuga** is an energetic age, although not a wise one. During this yuga, people are often self-serving and greedy. The age is marked by war and disease.

- **Kali Yuga** is the age of darkness, ignorance, and materialism. This is the least evolved age.

Today, The Holy Science is highly respected among those seeking to understand the relationships between world religions and cultures. While some still believe that we are in Kali Yuga, many others believe that Swami Sri Yukteswar was accurate, and that his calculations correct previous errors that artificially inflated the length of the Yuga Cycle.

कैवल्य दर्शनम्

THE HOLY SCIENCE

TABLE OF CONTENTS :-

Foreword by Sri Atul Chandra Chowdhury

Introduction

Chapter I : The Gospel

Chapter II : The Goal

Chapter II : The Procedure

Chapter IV : The Revelation

Conclusion

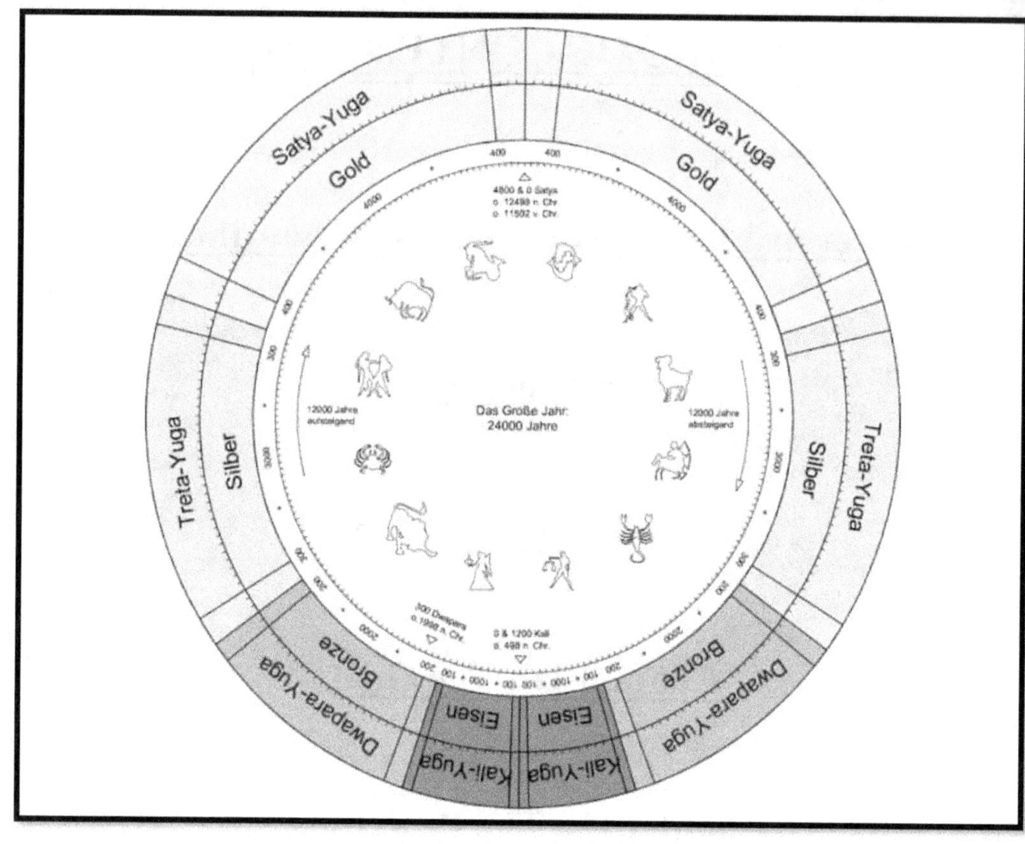

Satya-Yuga
Gold
Satya-Yuga
Gold
Treta-Yuga
Silber
Treta-Yuga
Silber
Bronze
Bronze
Dwapara-Yuga
Dwapara-Yuga
Eisen
Eisen
Kali-Yuga
Kali-Yuga
Das Große Jahr: 24000 Jahre
12000 Jahre aufsteigend
12000 Jahre absteigend

INTRODUCTION

चतुर्नवत्युत्तर शतवर्षे गते द्वापरस्य प्रयागक्षेत्रे ।

सदर्शनविज्ञानमन्वयार्थं परमगुरुराजस्याज्ञान्तु प्राप्य ॥

कड़ारवंश्यप्रियनाथस्वामिकादम्बिनीक्षेत्रनाथात्मजेन ।

हिताय विश्वस्य विदग्धतुष्टये प्रणीतं दर्शनं कैवल्यमेतत् ॥

The purpose of this present volume is to show as clearly as possible that there is an essential unity at the basis of all religions; that there is no difference in the truths inculcated by the various religions prevalent in the world, that there is but one method by which the world, both external and internal, has evolved; and that there is but one Goal admitted by all the religious books But it is not easy to comprehended this basic truth.

The discord existing between the different religions of the world and ignorance of men, make it almost impossible to lift the veil and have a look at this grand truth. The creeds keep up and faster the spirit of hostility and breed a feeling of perpetual dissension, and ignorance widens the gulf that separates one creed from another. Only a few specially gifted can rise superior to the influence of their professed creeds and find absolute unanimity in the truths propagated by all the religions of the world.

As the object of this book is to harmonize the different religions of the world and to bind them together. It will be create a real brotherhood among all the followers of all religions.

This is indeed a herculean task for a man like myself but I was entrusted with the mission by a holy command. Allahabad, the sacred *Prayaga Tirtha,* the place of confluence of the Ganges, jamuna and also of the intercurrent of the Saraswati. The kumbha mela is the congregation of worldly men and spiritual devotees.

The Worldly men cannot transcend the mundane limit which they confined themselves; nor the order having once renounced the world deign to come down and mix themselves with the turmoil of the world the world with its ordinary ways and with men wholly engrossed in worldly concerns stand in infinite need of help and guidance from those holy beings who bring light to the world.

So a place must there be where union between the two sets will be possible. *Tirtha* affords a meeting place. Situated as it is on the beach of the world, storms and buffets touch it not; the *sadhus* who have a message for the benefit of humanity have no difficulty before them to impart it to those who require it.

A message of such a nature I happened to be chosen to propagate when I paid a visit to the *Kumbha Mela* by my most revered Param Guru Deb. One day, as I was walking along the bank of the Ganges, I was called by a man and was afterwards honored by an interview with a great holy person, This holy personage was my *Param Guruji Maharaj,* I had a talk with him and our conversation turned up on the particular class of men who now frequent these places of pilgrimage.

I humbly suggested that there were men greater by far in intelligence than the men congregated there, living in distant nooks of the world—Europe and America— professing different creeds, and ignorant of the real significance of such *Mela as the present one.*

They were men fit to hold communion with spiritual devotees. But though they were men high in their intellectual attainments some of them were wedded to rank materialism. Some though famous for their investigations in the realms of science and philosophy did not recognize the essential unity in religion. The professed creeds served as insurmountable barriers that threatened to separate them from us forever.

My *Param Guruji Maharaj* Babaji smiled and, honoring me with the title of Swami, imposed this huge task upon me. I was chosen, I do not know the reason why, to remove this insurmountable barriers and to establish the real basic truth of religion.

The book is divided into four sections, according to the four stages in the development of knowledge. The highest end of religion is Atmajnanam (आत्मज्ञान) Self-knowledge. But to attain this the, knowledge of the external world is necessary.

So, the first section of the book deals with Veda (वेद:) the gospel, seeks to establish fundamental truths of creation and describe evolution and involution of the world.

Next, All creatures, from the highest to the lowest in the link of creation, are found eager to realize three things - Sat (सत्) Existence, Chitta (चित्) Consciousness, and Anand (आनन्द) Bliss. This is the purpose or goal of all creatures and so is the subject for discussion in the second section of the book.

The third section deals with Sadhana (साधना), the method to realize the three purposes of life. The subject which is discussed in the last section is Vibhuti (बिभूति), the revelations that come to those who have travelled far to realize the three ideals of life and are very near their destination.

The method I have adopted in the book is first to enunciate a proposition in Sanskrit terms of the Oriental sages, in form of Sutra (सूत्र) and then to explain it by reference to the holy scriptures of the West. In this way I tried my best to show that there is no real discrepancy, much less any real conflict, between the teachings of the East and the West. Written as the book is, under the inspiration of my *Param Gurudeva,* and in an Age of rapid development in all departments of knowledge, I hope that the significance of the book will not be missed by those for whom it is meant.

A short discussion with mathematical calculation of Yuga (युग) Era is necessary here in order to explain the fact that the present age is Dwapara Yuga, and 194 years of the Era is passed away, which is cause of this rapid development in all departments of knowledge.

We learn from Oriental astronomy that moons revolve around their planets, and planets turning on their axes revolve with their moon round the sun and the sun again, with its planets and their moons, tacking some star for its dual and revolve round each other in about 24,000 years of our earth—which causes the backward movement of the equinoxal points around the zodiac.

The sun also has another motion by which it revolves round a grand center called B*ishnunavi* (विष्णुनाभि) which is the seat of the creative power, *Brahma,* the universal magnetism. It informs us further that this Brahma the universal magnetism regulates *dharma,* the mental virtue of the internal world.

When the sun during its revolution round its dual comes to the place nearest to this grand centre, the seat of *Brahma -* this takes place when the Autumnal Equinox comes to the first point of Aries - this D*harma* the mental virtue, becomes so much developed that man can easily comprehend all, even the Spirit, beyond this visible world.

And after 12,000 years, when the sun goes to the place farthest from *this,* grand centre - which takes place when the Autumnal Equinox is on the first point of Libra - this *dharma,* the mental virtue, comes to such a reduced state that man cannot grasp anything beyond the gross material creation. Again, in the same manner, when the sun in its course of revolution begins to advance toward the place nearest to the grand centre, *dharma,* the mental virtue, begins to develop; this is gradually completed in another 12000 years.

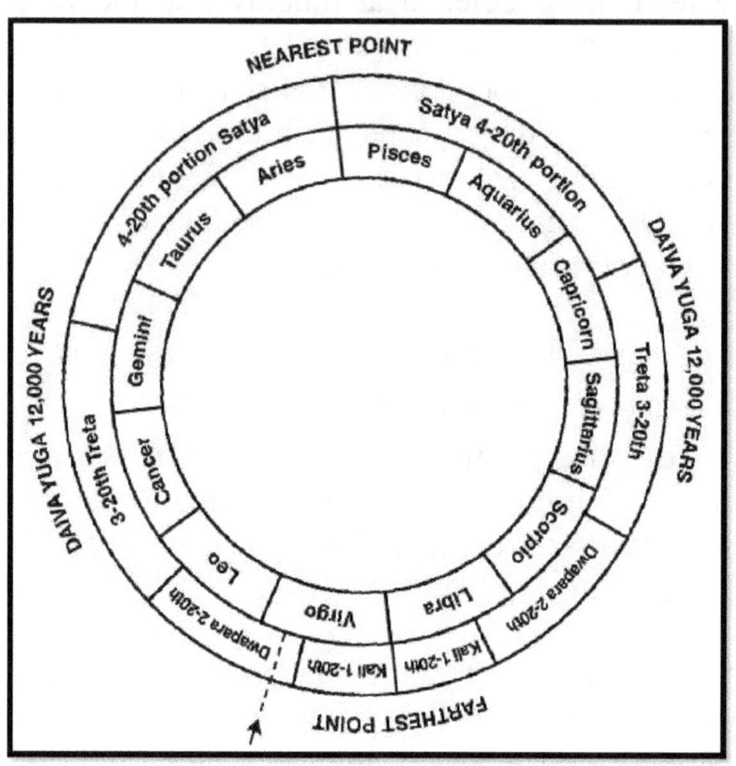

DIAGRAM

Each of these periods of 12,000 years brings a complete change, both externally in the material world, and internally in the intellectual or electric world, and is called one of the Daiba Yuga (दैव युग) or Electric Couple.

In a Couple of these Daiba Yugas extending over a period 24,000 of years, the sun completes the revolution round its dual and constitutes one electric cycle.

Development of *dharma,* the mental virtue, is but gradual and is divided into four different stages. So is the period of 24000 years which our sun takes to complete a revolution round, its dual divided into four yugas or couples of Era.

The period of 1200 years during which our sun passes through the 1/20th portion of its orbit of this revolution on either side of its point farthest from the grand centre (vide diagram) is called Kali yuga; *Dharma,* the mental virtue, being in the first stage is only a quarter developed and the human intellect cannot comprehend anything beyond the gross material of this ever changing creation the external world.

The period of 2400 years during which the sun passes through the 2/20th portion of its orbit, next to these on either side, is called Dwapara Yuga ; when *Dharma,* the mental virtue being in the second stage of development is but half complete and the human intellect can comprehend the fine matters or electricities and their attributes which are the creating principles of the external world.

The period of 3600 years during which the sun passes through the 3/20th the portion of its orbit is called Treta Yuga ; when *Dharma,* the mental virtue, being in the third stage; gradually completes the third quarter of its development and the human intellect becomes able to comprehend the magnetism, the source of electricities on which this creation depends for its existence.

And The period of 4800 years during which the sun passes through the remaining 4/20th portion of its orbit on either side of the point nearest to the grand centre, is called Satya Yuga; when *Dharma,* the mental virtue, is being in the fourth stage completes its full development; the husband intellect can comprehend all, even God the Spirit beyond this visible world.

Manu, a great R*ishi* of Satya Yuga, describes in his Samhita these Yugas more clearly in the following sloka :-

चत्वार्याहुः सहस्राणि वर्षाणान्तु कृतं युगम् ।
तस्य तावच्छती सन्ध्यां सन्ध्यांशश्च तथाविधः ॥

इतरेषु ससन्ध्येषु ससन्ध्यांशेषु च त्रिषु ।
एकापायेन वर्तन्ते सहस्राणि शतानि च ॥

यदेतत् परिसंख्यातमादावेव चतुर्युगम् ।
एतद् द्वादशसाहस्रं देवानां युगमुच्यते ॥

दैविकानां युगानान्तु सहस्रं परिसंख्यया ।
ब्राह्ममेकमहर्ज्ञेयं तावती रात्रिरेव च ॥

Four thousand year of our earth is the age of Satya Yuga and 4000 years previous to this period and 400 years and after it are its *sandhis* periods of mutation with the preceding and succeeding Yugas respectively; hence 4800 years in all is the proper age of Satya Yuga. In the calculation of the period of other Yugas and Yuga-sandhis, it is laid down that numerical one should be deducted from the numbers of thousands and hundreds indicating the periods of the previous Yugas and *sandhis.*

From this it appear that 3000 years is the age of Treta Yuga, and 300 years before and after are its *sandhis,* the mutation period, the periods of mutation, which make a total of 3600 years.

So 2000 years is the age of Dwapara Yuga, and 200 years before and after as its *sandhis;* a total of 2400 years. And lastly, 1000 years is the age of Kali Yuga, and 100 years before and after this period are its *sandhis;* a total of 1200 years.

Thus 12,000 years, the sum total of all periods of these four Yugas, is the age of one of the Daiba Yuga or Electric Couple, two of which, that is, 24,000 years, makes the electric cycle complete 1000 of such Daiba Yugas is the day of Brahma the creative power or Creator, when creation exists in manifested state; and the period equal to the above is its night when this creative power sleeps and the creation becomes dissolved.

From April 11501 B. C. when the Autumnal Equinox was on the first point of Aries, the sun began to move from the point of its orbit nearest to the grand centre towards the point farthest from it; and accordingly the intellectual power of man began to diminish. Till in 4800 years the sun took to pass through one of the Satya couples or 4/20th part of its orbit the intellect lost altogether the power of grasping the spiritual knowledge. During next 3600years after this, which the sun took to pass through one of the Treta couples or 3/20 part of its orbit more, the intellect gradually lost all its power of grasping the knowledge of the magnetism.

In next years more which the sun took to pass through one of the Dwapara couples or 2/20th part of its orbit, the intellect lost its power of grasping the knowledge of electricities and their attributes.

And in 1200 years more in April 499 A. D. when the sun passing through one of the Kali Yugas the remaining 1/20th part of its orbit reached to the point farthest from the grand centre, and the autumnal equinox was on the first point of Libra the intellectual power was so much diminished that it could no longer comprehend anything beyond the gross material of the creation.

This is what we commonly understand to be the darkest age of the Kali Yuga. From this time again the sun began to advance towards the grand centre and the intellectual power began to develop, the effect of which could be noticed in both the scientific and the political worlds.

After this darkest age of Kali Yuga during the next 1100 years which extended up to 1599 A. D. the human intellect was Electricities Sukshmabhuta (सूक्ष्मभूता), the fine matters of the creation and in the political world also, generally speaking there was no peace in any kingdom.

Subsequent to this, when Sandhi or time of mutation with Dwapara Yuga set in, men began to notice the existence of fine matters the attributes of electricities Panchatunmatra (पंचतन्मात्रा) and in the political world peace began to be established.

In about 1600 A. D. when Akbar the Emperor of Delhi established peace in India placing both the Hindus and Mahomedans on an equal footing, Queen Elizabeth of England brought to a close the continued struggle between the Protestants and the Roman catholics. Emperor Pojersky of Russia put an end to the Swedish disturbance in his Empire.

So in France, Italy, America and other parts of the world peace began to appear. In the Scientific world also in 1600 A. D., Gilbert discovered magnet and observed and asserted the existence of Electricity in all material substances.

In 1609 A D. Keplar discovered the laws in astronomy and Galileo discovered Telescope. In 1619 A. D. Solomon for the first time conceived the idea of Steam Engine. In 1621 A. D. Fortimer of Italy and Drabbel of Holland simultaneously discovered Microscope. In 1670 A. D. Hook and Newton discovered the law of gravitation about the same time. In this way did the science advance and from 1700 A. B. just after the Kali yuga had been over and the Sandhi or the time of mutation of the Dwapara yuga set in the Scientific theories were gradually reduced to practice, and they began to contribute much to the happiness of mankind.

In 1700 A. D. Captain Severy made use of Steam Engine in raising water. In 1720 A D. Stephen Grey discovered the action of Electricity on human system.

In 1766 A. D. Mesmer discovered the Art of healing with its assistance. In 1783 A. D. Joseph and Stephen ascended in balloon filled with hot air and after awhile Robert and Charles did the same with hydrogen gas.

And so again in the political world from about 1700 A. D. the people began to have respect for themselves; and civilization began to advance. Shivaji made an attempt to spread independence in India. Peter the Great ruled supreme in Russia. America began to establish independence. England united with Scotland became a powerful kingdom. At about 1100 A. D. when Lord Cornwallis made the permanent settlement in India, Napoleon Bonaparte introduced his new code in France, Spain, Italy & c. America was declared independent and similarly peace was almost permanently established in Russia, Venice, Sweden, Holland, Poland and all other parts of the world.

With the advancement of science also the world was adorned with railways, telegraphic wires and things of like nature. By the help of steam engines, electric machines and other instruments fine matters were brought into play although they were not clearly understood. After 1899 an the completion of the period of 200 years of Dwapara Sandhi the time of mutation, when the Dwapara proper will commence, the knowledge of the aforesaid fine matters will begin to develop and in a few years more will become so very common place that it will come within the reach of the people in general.

Such is the great influence of Time which governs the universe. No man can overcome this influence except he who, blessed with pure love, the heavenly gift of nature, becomes divine; being baptized in the stream Pranava (प्रणव) comprehends the Kingdom of God.

Now in this 1894 A. D. the dark age of Kali yuga having long passed away, in this 194th year of Dwapara when the people growing anxious for the spiritual knowledge and feeling for the same requires help of each other and reciprocate love between them, the introduction of this book to the public will, I hope, not be untimely.

But a great mistake has crept in the calculation of these yugas in our almanac of present age. The astronomers as well as the astrologers of this age, without caring much for the proper method of calculating the same, having been guided by Some wrong annotation of some of the Sanskrit scholars such as Kullu Bhatta & co. of the dark age of Kali yuga maintain that the age of Kali yuga is 432000 years of which 4994 only have passed away and 427006 years still remaining.

This mistake crept into the almanac for the first time in the reign of Raja Parikshita the grandson of Maharaja Yudhisthir just after the completion of the Dwapara yuga when Maharaja Yudhisthir noticing the appearance of the dark Kali yuga made over his throne to his grandson the said Raja Parikshit and retired with his brothers to the top of the Himalaya mountain the paradise of the world. The wise men of his Court followed him in his retirement. Thus there was none in the Court of Raja Parikshit who could understand the principle of correctly calculating the ages of the several yugas.

Hence after the completion of 2400 years of the then current Dwapara yuga, none dared to make the introduction of putting a stop to the number of years then current.

According to the calculation, therefore, the first year of Kali were numbered 2400 along with the age of Dwapara. So in 499 A. D. when 1200 years the age of Kali was complete, and the sun reached the point of its orbit farthest from the grand centre - when the autumnal equinox was on the first point of its Libra - the age of Kali in its darkest period was then numbered by 3600 years instead of by 1200.

With the commencement of the second one of the couple of Kali, the sun began to advance towards the point nearest the grand Centre, and accordingly to what has already been said, the intellectual power of man began to develop.

In course of a few years more, however, the mistake thus introduced into the calculation began to be noticed by the wise men of the time; who found according to the calculation of the ancient Rishis the age of Kali Yuga was fixed at 1200 years only.

But as the intellect of these wise men was not yet suitably developed, they could not make out the reason for the mistake beyond the mistake itself; and by way of reconciliation they fancied that 1200 years, the real age of Kali, were not the ordinary years of our earth; but they were so many Daiba years consisting of 12 Daiba months of 30 Daiba days each and each Daiba day being again equal to one ordinary year of our earth. Hence according to them 1200 years of Kali are equal to 432000 years of our earth.

In coming to a right conclusion, however, we should take into consideration the position of the vernal equinox on the 22nd April 1893 A. D. the beginning of this equinoctial year ;

and the astronomical observation will show that it is 20Â°-54'-36" in advance of the first point of Aries, and by calculation it will appear that 1394 years have passed away since the time when the vernal equinox began to advance from the first point of Aries. Deducting, therefore, 1200 years (which completed the second one of the couple of Kali) from that period, the remaining 194 years indicate the present age of Dwapara yuga.

The mistake above referred to will therefore be clearly explained when we add 3600 years to this 1394 years and get 4994 years, which according to the mistaken theory represent the present age of Kali yuga in the Almanac.

In should be mentioned here that some of the truths such as the properties of magnet its aura, different sorts of electricity & c have been mentioned in this book, although they are not yet fully discovered.

As for the five sorts of electricity, however, it may be mentioned that they can be easily understood if one would direct his attention to the nerve properties which are nothing but purely electric. The five sensory nerve have got their peculiar functions respectively to perform. Such as optic nerve carries light and does not perform the functions of auditory and other nerves and auditory nerve in its turn carries sound only without performing the functions of any other nerves and so on. Thus it is clear that there are five sorts of electricity corresponding to the aforesaid five properties which enable these five sorts of sensory nerves to perform their peculiar functions by carrying five different objects of sense respectively.

So far as magnetic properties are concerned, it may be remembered that the grasping power of the human intellect, as at present stands, is so limited that it would be quite useless to attempt to make it understood by the general public.

The ordinary people of this *yuga* whose intellect, accordingly to what has already been said, will be suitably developed in course of 2000 years, when the period of mutation with *Tretayuga* will set in.

- Swami Sri Yukteswar Giri

CHAPTER 1
वेद: THE GOSPEL

वेद

SUTRA 1

नित्यं पूर्णमनाद्यनन्तं ब्रह्म परम् ।

तदेवैकमेवाद्वैतं सत् । १ ।

The Eternal Father, God, *Swami Parambrahma,* is the only Real Substance, *Sat in unit,* and is all in all in the universe.

'God' Swami' why not comprehensible :

Man has got eternal faith and believes intuitively in the existence of a Substance, of which the objects of sense — sound, touch, sight, taste, and small, the component parts of this visible world — are but properties. As man identifies himself with his material body, composed of the aforesaid properties, he is able to comprehend by his imperfect organs these properties only, and not the Substance to which these properties belong. The Eternal Father God, the only Substance in the universe, is therefore not comprehensible by man of this material world, unless he becomes divine by lifting his self above this creation of Darkness Maya. Vide Hebrew XI. I. John VIII. 28

"Now faith is the substance of things hoped for, the evidence of things not seen."

तत्र सर्वज्ञप्रेमबीजञ्चित् सर्वशक्तिबीजमानन्दश्च ॥ २ ॥

"Then said Jesus unto them, When ye have lifted up the son of man, then shall ye know that I am he."

Prakriti THE Nature :

The Almighty Force, *Shakti,* or in other word the Eternal Joy, *Ananda,* which produces the world; and the Omniscient Feeling, *Chit,* which makes this world conscious, demonstrate the Nature, *Prakriti,* of God the Father.

How comprehended :

As man is the likeness of God, directing his attention inward he can comprehend within him the said Force and Feeling, the sole properties of his Self—the Force Almighty as his will, B*asana,* which enjoyment, *Bhoga;* and the Feeling Omniscient as his Consciousness, *Chetana,* that enjoys, *Bhokta.* Vide *Genesis* 1.27

"So God created man in his own image, in the image of God created he him; male and female created he them."

तत्सर्वशक्तिबीजजडप्रकृतिवासनाया व्यक्तभावः ।
प्रणवशब्दः दिक्कालाण्वोऽपि तस्य रूपाणि ॥ ३ ॥

The Word, *Amen (Aum),* is the beginning of the Creation.

The manifestation of Omnipotent Force (the Repulsion its complementary portion, Omniscient Feeling - Love, the Attraction) is vibration, which appears as a peculiar sound; the Word (शब्द) *Amen Aum.*

The Four Aspects : The Word, Time, Space, and Atom.

And in its different aspects presents the idea of change, which is Time, *Kal,* (काल) in the Ever- Unchangeable; and the idea of division, which is Space, *Desh (देश),* in the Ever-indivisible, the effect whereof is the idea of particles the innumerable atoms patra or anu. (अणु) These four viz. the Word, Time, Space and Atom, therefore, are one and the same and substantially nothing but mere ideas.

This manifestation the Word (becoming flesh, the external material) created this visible world. So the Word, *Amen, Aum,* being the manifestation of the Eternal Nature of the Almighty Father on His Own Self, is inseparable from and nothing but God Himself; as the burning power is inseparable from and nothing but the fire itself. Vide rewv111,14 *John* 1.1, 3, 14.

"These things saith Amen, the faithful and true witness, the beginning of the creation.

"In the beginning was the Word, the Word was with God, and the Word was God.…

All things were made by him; and without him was not anything made that was made.…

And the Word was made flesh and dwelt among us. :-"

तदेव जगत्कारणं माया ईश्वरस्य, तस्य व्यष्टिरविद्या ॥ ४ ॥

Atoms the throne of the Creator.

These Atoms, which represent within and without the four ideas mentioned above, are the throne of Spirit, the Creator, that shining on them creates this universe. They are called en masse *Maya,* the Darkness, as they keep the Spiritual Light out of comprehension; and each of them separately is called *Avidya,* the Ignorance, as it makes man ignorant even of his own Self.

Hence the aforesaid four ideas which give rise to all those confusions are mentioned in the Bible as so many beasts. Man, so long as he identifies himself with his gross material body, holds a position far inferior to that of the Atom and necessarily fails to comprehend the same. But when he raises himself to the level thereof, he not only comprehends this Atom, both inside and outside, but also the creation before - arising out of it, and that behind - which precedes the same. Vide Revelation IV. 6

"And in the midst of the throne, and round about the throne, were four beasts full of eyes before and behind."

तत्सर्वज्ञप्रेमबीजं परं तदेव कूटस्थचैतन्यम् ।
पुरुषोत्तमः तस्याभासः पुरुषः तस्मादभेदः । ५ ।

Kutastha Chaitanya, the Holy Ghost, *Purushottama.*

The manifestation of Prembhijam chit attraction omniscient love, is life the omnipresent holy spirit and is called the ghost kutashta chaitnaya or *Premabijam Chit* (Attraction, the Omniscient Love) is Life, the Omnipresent Holy Spirit, and is called the Holy Ghost, *Kutastha Chaitanya* or *Purushottama,* which shines on the Darkness, *Maya,* to attract every portion of it toward Divinity. But the Darkness, *Maya,* or its individual parts, *Avidya* the Ignorance, being repulsion itself, cannot receive or comprehend the Spiritual Light, but reflects it.

Avas-Chaitanya or *Purush,* the Son of God.

This Holy Ghost, being the manifestation of the Omniscient Nature of the Eternal Father, God, is no other substance than God Himself; and so these reflections of spiritual rays are called the Sons of God—*Avasa (Abhasa) Chaitanya* or *Purusha vide John* I. 4, 5, 11.

"In him was life; and the life was the light of men.

"And the light shineth in darkness; and the darkness comprehended it not."

"He came unto his own, received his own received him not."

चित्सकाशादणोर्महत्त्वं तच्चित्तम्, तत्रसदध्यवसायः ।

सत्त्वं बुद्धिः ततस्तद्विपरीतं मनः

चरमेऽभिमानोऽहंकारस्तदेव जीवः । ६ ।

Chittwa The Heart, *Ego,*

Ahamkar, the Son of Man

Buddhi, the Intelligence

Manas, the Mind

This Atom, *Avidya,* the Ignorance, being under the influence of Universal Love, *Chit,* the Holy Spirit, becomes spiritualized, like iron filings in a magnetic aura, and possessed of consciousness, the power of feeling, when it is called *Mohot,* the Heart, *chittwa;* and being such the idea of separate existence of self appears in it, which is called *Ahamkara,* Ego, the son of man.

Thus being polarised it gets two poles, one of which attracts it toward the Real Substance, *Sat,* and the other repels it from the same. The former is called *Sattwa* or *Buddhi,* the Intelligence, which determines what is Truth; and the latter, being a particle of Repulsion, the Almighty Force spiritualized as aforesaid, produces the ideal world for enjoyment *ananda* and is called *Anandatwa* or *Manas,* the Mind.

तदहंकारचित्तविकारपञ्चतत्त्चानि । ७ ।

तान्येव कारणशरीरं पुरुषस्य । ८ ।

तेषां त्रिगुणेभ्यः पञ्चदश विषयेन्द्रियाणि । ९ ।

एतानि मनोबुद्धिभ्यां सह सप्तदशसूक्ष्मांगानि ।

लिंगशरीरस्य । ९० ।

7-10. This spiritualized Atom, *chittwa* (the Heart), being the Repulsion manifested produces five sorts of aura - electricities - from its five different parts : one from the middle, two from the two extremities, and the other two from the spaces intervening between the middle and each of the extremities.

Pancha Tattwa, the Root-Causes of creation, is the causal body.

These five sorts of electricities being attracted under the influence of Universal Love (the Holy Ghost) toward the Real Substance, *Sat,* produce a magnetic field which is called the body of *sattwa Buddhi,* the Intelligence.

These five electricities being the causes of all other creations are called *Pancha-Tattwa,* the five Root-Causes, and named as Causal body of Purush the Son of God.

Three *Gunas,* the electric attributes.

The electricities, being evolved from the polarized *chittwa* are also in a polarized state and are endowed with its three attributes *Gunas-Sattwa* the positive, *Tama* the negative, and *Rajas* the neutralizing attributes.

Jnyanendriyas, the five organs of the senses.

The positive attributes of these five electricities are Jnyanendriyas the organs of sense—organs of smell, taste, sight, touch and hearing— and being attracted under the influence of manas Mind the opposite pole of this Spiritualised Atom constitutes a body of the same.

Karmendriyas, the five organs of action.

The neutralising attributes of them are Karmendriyas the organs of action—those of excretion, generation, motion, absorption, and articulation. These organs being the manifestation of the neutralising energy of the Spiritualised Atom Chittwa the Heart constitutes an energetic body called the body of energy the life Pran.

Bishaya or Tanmatras, the five objects of the senses.

And their negative attributes of the five objects of senses and smell, taste, sight, touch, and sound, which, through the neutralizing power of the organs of action, being the united with the organs of sense satiate the desires of the heart.

Lingasarira, the fine material body.

These fifteen attributes with two poles—Mind and Intelligence—of the spiritualized Atom constitute *Lingasarira* or *Sukshma-sarira,* the fine material body of *Purush,* the Son of God.

तततः पञ्चतत्त्चानां स्थितिशीलतामसिकविषयपञ्चतन्मात्राणां

पञ्चीकरणेन स्थूलशरीरस्यांगानि जडीभूतपञ्चक्षित्यप्तेजो

मरुद्व्योमान्युद्भूतानि । ११ ।

एतान्येव चतुर्विंशतिः तत्त्चानि । १२ ।

Gross material body.

11-12. The aforesaid five objects, which are the negative attributes of the five electricities, being combined together produce the idea of the gross matters which appear to us in five different varie- ties viz. Kshiti the Solid Ap the Liquid Tej the subgaseous Marut the gaseous Gross-material body, and Byoma or Akasha the Ethereal and constitute the outer covering called Sthulsharir the gross material body of Purush the son of God.

Twenty-four Elders.

These five gross matters and the aforesaid fifteen attributes together with Manas the Mind. Buddhi the Intelligence, Chittwa the Heart and Ahamkar the Ego, constitute the twenty-four principles Elders as mentioned in the Bible. Vide Rev. IV 4.

"And round about the throne were four and twenty seats; and upon the seats I saw four and twenty elders."

The aforesaid twenty four principles which completed the creation of Darkness Maya are nothing but mere development of Ignorance Abidya; and this Ignorance being composed only of ideas as mentioned above, this creation has no substantial existence in reality but is mere play of ideas on the Eternal Substance God the Father.

तत्रैव चतुर्दशभुवनानि व्याख्यातानि । १३ ।

Seven Spheres or *Swargas*

This universe thus described commencing from the Eternal Substance God down to the gross material creation has been distinguished into seven different spheres, Swargas or Lokas.

7th Sphere, *Satyaloka*

The foremost of these is Satyaloka the sphere of God the only Real Substance Sat in the universe. No name can describe nor anything in the creation of Darkness or Light can designate it. Because this sphere is called Anam the Nameless. II.

The next in order is Tapaloka the sphere of the Holy Spirit which is the 6th Sphere Tapaloka Eternal Patience as it re- mains for ever undisturbed by any limited idea; and because it is not approachable even by the Son of God as such it is called Agam the Inaccessible.

6th Sphere, *Tapoloka*

The next in order is Tapaloka the sphere of the Holy Spirit which is the Eternal Patience as it remains forever undisturbed by any limited idea; and because it is not approachable even by the Son of God as such it is called Agam the Inaccessible.

5th Sphere, *Janaloka*

Next is Janaloka the sphere of Spiritual reflection the sons of God where in the idea of separate existence of Self originates. As this sphere is above the comprehension of any body, in the creation of Darkness, Maya, it is called Alakhsa the Incomprehensible.

4th Sphere, *Maharloka*

Then comes Maharloka, the sphere of Atom, the beginning of the creation of Darkness Maya upon which the Spirit is reflected. This being the connecting link this is the only way between the Spiritual and material creation and is called the Door Dasamadwar.

3rd Sphere

Around this Atom is Sivaloka the sphere of magnetic aura, the electricities, This sphere being characterized by the absence of all the creation even the organs and its objects the fine material things is called Mahashunya the great Vacuum.

2nd Sphere, *Bhubaloka*

The next is Bhubaloka the electric attributes. As the gross matters of the creation are entirely absent from this sphere and it is conspicuous by the presence of the fine matters only it is called Shunya the vacuum ordinary.

1st Sphere, *Bhuloka*

The last and lowest sphere is Bhuloka the sphere of gross material creation, which is always visible to everybody.

Sapta Patalas, or seven churches.

As God created Man in his own image, so is the body of Man like into the image, of this universe. The material body of Man has also got seven conspicuous places within it called Patals. Turning towards his self while man advances in the right way he perceives the Spiritual Light in these places which are described in the Bible as so many Churches and the Lights perceived therein like stars as so many Angels. Vide Rev. I. 12, 13, 16, 20.

"And having turned, I saw seven golden candlesticks, and in the midst of the seven candlesticks one like into the son of man...."

"And he had in his right hand seven stars...."

"The seven stars are the angels of the seven churches; and the seven candlesticks which thou sawest are the seven churches."

14 *Bhuvanas,* the stages of creation.

The above-mentioned Seven Spheres or Swargas and seven Patals constitutes the Fourteen Bhubans the fourteen distinguished stages of the creation.

त एव पञ्च कोषाः पुरुषस्य । ९४ ।

Five *koshas* or sheaths

This Purush the Son of God is screened by five fold of coverings called Koshas Sheaths.

Heart, the 1st *Kosha*

The first of these five is Heart Chittwa the Atom composed of four ideas as mentioned before which feels or enjoys and thus being the seat of enjoyment ananda is called Anandamoya Kosha.

Aura, the 2nd *Kosha.*

The second is the magnetic aura electricities manifestations of Buddhi the intelligence which determines what is truth.

Thus being the seat of knowledge jnyan is called jnyanamoya Kosha.

Manas, the 3rd *Kosha*

The third is the body of Manas the Mind composed of the organs of sense as mentioned above and is called the Manamaya Kosha.

Prana, the 4th *Kosha*

The fourth is the body of energy the life Pran composed of the organs of action as described before and so is called the Pranamaya kosha.

Gross-matters the 5th *Kosha*

The fifth and the last of these sheaths is the gross matter the Atom's outer coating which becoming Anna the nourishment supports this visible world, and thus is called the Annamoya Kosha.

Action of Love
Inanimate kingdom

The action of Repulsion the manifestation of the Omnipotent Energy being thus completed, the action of Attraction the manifestation of the Omniscient Love in the core of the heart begins to be manifested. Under this influence of this Omniscient Love the attraction, the Atoms being attracted towards each other, comes nearer and nearer taking the forms of Ethereal Gaseous, Sub Gaseous, Liquid and Solid adorns this visible world with suns, stars, planets, moons & c which we perceive as inanimate Kingdom in the creation.

Vegetable kingdom

In this manner when the action of the Divine Love becomes well-developed, the evolution of Avidya Ignorance the particle of Darkness Maya the Omnipotent Energy manifested, begins to be withdrawn.

And thus Annamoya Kosha the Atom's outer coating of gross matter being withdrawn Pranamaya Kosha the sheath composed of Karmendria the organs of action transpires. In this organic state the Atoms embracing each other more close to their heart appears to us as vegetable kingdom in the creation.

Animal kingdom

In this way when the aforesaid Pranamaya Kosha becomes withdrawn, the Manamaya Khosa the sheath composed of jnyanendrias the organs of sense comes to the light, and being so the Atoms perceives the nature of the external world and attracting other atoms of different nature forms its body for enjoyment as necessary and thus appears to us as animal Kingdom in the creation.

Mankind

Thus after taking several forms of body when Manamaya Kosha the sheath aforesaid becomes withdrawn Jnyanamaya Kosha the body of Intelligence composed of electricities becomes perceptible and the Atom getting the power of determining right and wrong becomes man the rational being in the creation.

Devata or Angel

When man cultivating the Divine Spirit - Omniscient Love - within his heart can make this Jnyanamaya Kosha the sheath of Intelligence withdrawn the innermost sheath Chittwa the Heart composed of four ideas - the Holy Sound, Amen Aum & c becomes manifested then he is called Debata Angel, in the creation.

Free, *Sannyasi.*

Thus when Heart the innermost sheath is also withdrawn these being nothing to help the man in the bondage of this creation of Darkness Maya he becomes free Sannyasi the Son of God and enters into the creation of Light.

स्थूलज्ञानक्रमात् सूक्ष्मविषयेन्द्रियज्ञानं स्वप्नवत् । १५ ।

तत्क्रमात् मनोबुद्धिज्ञानञ्चायातमिति परोक्षम् । १६ ।

15-16. When man compares his ideas relating to gross matters conceived in wakeful state with his conception of ideas in dream, the similarity existing between them naturally leads him to conclude this external world also is not what it appears to be, and when he looks for further explanation he finds that the conception thereof is substantially nothing but mere ideas caused by the union of five objects of sense-the negative attributes of the five internal electricities -with the five organs of sense their positive attributes-through the medium of five organs of action-the neutralizing attributes thereof.

This union is affected by the operation of Mind Manas and conceived by the Intelligence Buddhi. Thus it is clear the conceptions so arrived at are mere inferential *Parokshajnyan*—a matter of inference only.

तत: सद्गुरुलाभो भक्तियोगश्च तेनापरोक्ष: । १७ ।

When Man Get *Sat-Guru, the Preceptor*

In this way, when man understands by his Parakshajnyan the nothingness of the external world, he appreciates the position of the Divine personage who witnessed Light and bears testimony of Christ and his heart's love, the heavenly gift of Nature, becomes developed.

Then he may be fortunate in having the God like company of some one of such personages who may kindly stand to him as his Spiritual Preceptor, Sat Guru, the Saviour.

Following affectionately the holy precepts of these divine personages, man becomes able to direct all his organs inward to their common centre-Sensorium, Trikuti or Sushumna-dwar, the door of the interior, where he comprehends the voice, like a peculiar knocking sound the Word Amen, Aum, and the God sent luminous body of Radha, called John in the Bible. Vide Rev. III, 14, 20. John I. 6, 8, 23.

"These things saith the Amen, the faithful and true witness, the beginning of the creation."

"Behold, I stand at the door, and knock; if any man hear my voice and open the door, I will come in to him and will sup with him, and he with me."

"There was a man sent from God, whose name was John...."

"He was not that Light, but was sent to bear witness of that Light...."

"He said, I am the voice of one crying in the wilderness, Make straight the way of the Lord is said the prophet Esaias."

Ganga, Jumna, or Jordan, the holy streams.

From the peculiar nature of this sound ensuing as it does like a stream from a the holy Stream, Ganga Jumna or Jordan higher unknown region and loses itself in the gross material creation, it is figuratively styled by different sects of people by the names of different rivers which they consider as sacred; e.g. Ganga by the Aryans, Jumna by the Baishnavs, Jordon by the Christians & c.

Baptization the 2nd Birth.

Through this luminous body, John, man believing in the existence of the true Light - the Life of this universe becomes baptized or absorbed in the holy stream of the sound. This Baptization is, so to speak, the second birth of man and is called, Bhakti yoga, without which man can never become able to comprehend the real position of internal world, the Kingdom of God. Vide, John I, 9. III 3.

"That was the true Light, which lighteth every man that cometh into the world."

"Verily, verily, I say unto thee, Except a man be born again, he   cannot see the kingdom of God."

Aparoksha Jnyan the real comprehension.

In this state the Son of Man begins to repent (Lat. Repens to creep) and turning back from the gross real comprehension. material creation creeps toward his Divinity, the Eternal Substance, God: when the development of Ignorance begins to recede, and man gradually comprehends the true character of this creation of Darkness, Maya, as mere ideal play of the Supreme Nature on his own self, the only Real Substance. This comprehension is called Aparokshajnyan.

यदात्मनः परमात्मनि दर्शनन्ततः कैवल्यम् । १८ ।

Sannyasi or Christ the anointed Savior.

When all the developments of Ignorance are withdrawn, the Heart being perfectly clear and purified no longer reflects the Spiritual Light but receives the same and thus being consecrated and anointed becomes Sannyasi or Christ the Saviour. Vide John I, 33.

"Upon whom thou shalt see the Spirit descending, and remaining on him, the same is he which baptizeth with the Holy Ghost."

Through this Saviour, the Son of man becomes again baptised or absorbed in the stream of Spiritual Light and coming above the creation of Darkness, Maya enters into the Spiritual world and becomes unified with Abhas Chaitanya or Purush, the Son of God, as was the case with Lord Jesus of Nazareth mentioned in the Bible. This was the state when man is saved forever and ever from the bondage of Darkness Maya. Vide John, I, 12, III, 5.

"But as many as received him, to them gave he power to become the Sons of God, even to them that believe on his name."

"Verily, verily, I say unto thee, except a man be born of water and of the Spirit, he cannot enter into the kingdom of God."

Sacrifice of self.

When man, thus entering into the Spiritual world, becomes Son of God he comprehends the universal Light- the Holy Ghost-as a perfect whole, and his self as nothing but a mere idea resting on a fragment thereof.

Then he sacrifices himself to Holy Ghost the altar of God i.e. abandons the vain idea of his separate existence and becomes one integral whole with the same.

Kaivalya, the Unification.

Thus being one and the same with universal Holy Spirit of God the Father, he becomes unified with the Real Substance, God, in no time. This unification of self with the Eternal substance, God, is called Kaibalya Vide Rev. III. 21.

"To him that overcometh will I grant to sit with me in my throne, even as I also overcame, and am sat down with my Father in his throne."

CHAPTER - 2

THE GOAL

अभीष्टम्।

अतो मुक्तिजिज्ञासा । १ ।

1. Liberation, the prime object.

When man understands even by way of inference the true nature of this creation, the true relation existing between that creation and himself, when he further understands that he is completely blinded by the influence of Darkness, - Maya, and that it is the bondage of Darkness alone which makes him forget his real self and brings about all his sufferings, he naturally wishes to be relieved from all these evils, and this relief from evil or the liberation from the bondage of Darkness, Maya, becomes the prime object of his life.

मुक्तिः स्वरूपेऽवस्थानम् । २ ।

2. Residing in Self in liberation.

When man raises himself above the idea creation of this Darkness, *Maya,* and passes completely out of its influence thereof, he becomes liberated from bondage and is placed in his real Self, the Eternal Spirit.

तदा सर्वक्लेशनिवृत्तिः परमार्थसिद्धिश्च । ३ ।

3.Liberation is salvation.

On attaining this liberation, man becomes saved from all his troubles, and all the desires of his heart are fulfilled, so the ultimate aim of his life is accomplished.

इतरत्र अपूर्णकामजन्मजन्मान्तरव्यापि दुःखम् । ४ ।

4. Why man suffers.

So long, however, as man identifies himself with his material body and fails to find repose in his true Self, he feels his wants according as his heart's desires remain unsatisfied and to satisfy which he has to appear in flesh and blood often enough, on the stage of life, subject to the influence of Darkness, *Maya,* and has to suffer all the troubles of life and death not only in the present but in the future as well.

क्लेशोऽविद्यामातृकः । ५ ।

भावेऽभावोऽभावे भाव इत्येवं बोधोऽविद्या । ६ ।

5-6. What is ignorance?

Ignorance, *Abidya* is misconception, or is the erroneous conception of existence of that which does not exist. It is to believe that this material creation is the only thing which substantially exists, there being nothing beyond, forgetting that this material creation is substantially nothing but is mere play of ideas on the Eternal Spirit, the only Real Substance, beyond the comprehension of the material creation. This Ignorance is not only a trouble in itself but also the source of all the other troubles with man.

तदेवावरणविक्षेपशक्तिविशिष्टत्वात्
क्षेत्रमस्मिताभिनिवेशरागद्वेषाणाम् । ७ ।
तस्यावरणशक्तेरस्मिताभिनिवेशौ विक्षेपशक्तेश्च रागद्वेषौ । ८ ।
स्वामिशक्त्योरविविक्तज्ञानमस्मिता । ९ ।
प्राकृतिकसंस्कारमात्रमभिनिवेशः । १० ।
सुखकरविषयतृष्णा रागः । ११ ।
दुःखकरविषयत्यागतृष्णा द्वेषः । १२ ।

7-12. Ignorance is the source of all troubles.

In order to understand how this Ignorance is the source of all other troubles we should remember as has been explained in the previous chapter that Ignorance, *Abidya,* is nothing but a particle of Darkness, *Maya,* taken distributively, and as such it possesses the two properties thereof, The one is its darkening power by the influence of which man is prevented from grasping anything beyond the material creation. This darkening power produces *Asmita* or Egoism, the identification of Self with the material body, which is but the development of Atom, the particles of the universal force; and *Avinibesha* or Tenacity to the Condition.

By the virtue of the second of its properties, this Ignorance in its polarized state produces an attraction for certain objects and repulsion for others. The objects so attracted are the objects of pleasure, for which an Attachment, *Raga,* is produced. The objects that are repulsed are the objects producing pain, for which an Aversion, *Dwesha,* is produced.

क्लेशमूलं कर्म तद्विपाक एव दुःखम् । १३ ।

13. Why man works.

By the influence of these five troubles—Ignorance, Egotism, Attachment, Aversion, and Tenacity to the material creation—man is induced to works and in consequence he suffers.

सर्वदुःखानां निवृत्तिरित्यर्थः । १४ ।

निवृत्तावप्यनुवृत्त्यभावः परमः । १५ ।

14-15. Ultimate aim of the heart.

With man the cessation of all suffering is *Artha,* the heart's immediate aim. The complete extirpation of all these sufferings, their recurrence being impossible, is *Paramartha,* the ultimate goal.

सर्वकामपूर्णत्वे सर्वदुःखमूलक्लेशनिवृत्तिः तदा

परमार्थसिद्धिः । १६ ।

सच्चिदानन्दमयत्वप्राप्तिरिति स्थिरकामाः । १७ ।

सद्गुरुदत्तसाधनप्रभावात् चित्तस्य प्रसाद एवानन्दः । १८ ।

ततः सर्वदुःखानां हानन्तदा सर्वभावोदयश्चित् । १९ ।

तत आत्मनो नित्यत्वोपलब्धिः सत् । २० ।

तदेव स्वरूपं पुरुषस्य । २१ ।

16-21. The real necessities.

Man naturally feels great necessity for *Sat,* Existence; *Chit,* Consciousness; and *Ananda,* Bliss. These three are the real necessities of the human heart which however have nothing to do with anything outside his Self. They are the natural properties of his own, as explained in the previous chapter.

How man gets Bliss.

When man becomes fortunate in securing the favor of any divine personage, *Sat-Guru* the Savior, and affectionately following his holy precepts, becomes able to direct all his organ inward, he becomes capable of satisfying all the wants of his heart and can thereby get contentment, *Ananda,* the Real Bliss, Which will be explained hereafter.

How Consciousness appears.

With his heart thus contented, man becomes able to fix his attention upon anything he chooses and can comprehend the ins and outs of the same. So *Chit,* Consciousness of all the modifications of Nature up to its first manifestation, the Word Amen, *Aum,* and even of his own Real Self, gradually appears. And being absorbed in the stream thereof, man becomes baptized and begins to repent toward his Divinity the Eternal Father, whence he had fallen. Vide *Revelation* Chap II, 5:--

"Remember therefore from whence thou art fallen, and repent."

How Existence is realized.

Man, being conscious of his own real position and of the nature of this creation of Darkness, *Maya,* becomes possessed of absolute power over it, and gradually withdraws all the developments of Ignorance. In this way, coming above the control of this creation of Darkness Maya, he comprehends his own Self as Indestructible and Ever-Existing Real Substance. So *Sat,* the Existence of Self, comes to light.

How main object of the heart is attained.

All the necessities of the heart—Viz. *Sat,* Existence; *Chit,* Consciousness; and *Ananda,* Bliss—having been attained, Ignorance, the mother of troubles becomes emaciated ; and consequently all troubles of this material world, which are the sources of all sorts of sufferings, cease forever. Thus the ultimate aim of the heart is affected.

तदा सर्वकामपूर्णोपरमार्थसिद्धिकात् गुणानाम्प्रतिप्रसव

आत्मनः स्वरूपप्रतिष्ठा, तदेव कैवल्यम् । २२ ।

How man finds salvation.

In this state, all the necessities having been attained and the ultimate aim effected, the heart becomes perfectly purified and, instead of reflecting the spiritual light receives the same; and thus being consecrated or anointed by the Holy Spirit, becomes Christ, the anointed Saviour through which man entering into the kingdom of Spiritual Light becomes the Son of God.

In this state man comprehends his Self as a fragment of the Universal Holy Spirit, and abandoning the vain idea of his separate existence, unifies himself with the Eternal Spirit; that is, becomes one and the same with God the Father. This unification of Self with God is *Kaivalya,* which is the Ultimate Object of the created being. Vide *John* XIV, II.

"Believe me that I am in the Father, and the Father in me."

CHAPTER 3

THE PROCEDURE

साधन ।

तपःस्वाध्यायब्रह्मनिधानानि यज्ञः । १ ।

मात्रास्पर्शेषु तितिक्षा तपः । २ ।

आत्मतत्त्वोपदेशश्रवणमनननिदिध्यासनमेव स्वाध्यायः । ३ ।

प्रणवशब्द एव पन्था ब्रह्मणः तस्मिन् आत्मसमर्पणं ब्रह्मनिधानम् । ४ ।

1-4. Patience, Faith, and Holy works explained.

Tapas is religious mortification or patience both in enjoyments and sufferings. *shadhyaya* is shraban the study, with manan the attention, and thereby *nidhidhyasan;* forming of an idea of the true Faith about Self; that is, what I am, whence I came, where shall I go, what I have come for, and such other matters concerning Self. *Brahmanidhan* is the Baptization or merging of Self in the stream of the Holy Sound (*Pranava,*), which is the holy work to attain salvation and the only way by which man can repent to his Divinity, the Eternal Father, whence he had fallen vide Rev. 11:19.

"I know thy works, and charity and service, and thy faith, and thy patience, and thy work; and the last to be more than the first."

श्रद्धावीर्यस्मृतिसमाध्यनुष्ठानात् तस्याविर्भावः । ५ ।

स्वभावजप्रेम्णः वेगतीव्रता श्रद्धा । ६ ।

How the Holy Sound appears. This Holy Sound *Pranava Sabda* appears it self by culture of *Sraddha,* the energetic tendency of heart's natural love; veerya the, moral courage; *Smriti,* true conception; and *Samadhi,* the concentration.

The virtue of Love. The heart's natural love is the principal thing to attain a holy life. When this love, the heavenly gift of Nature, appears in the heart, it removes all exciting causes from the system and cools it down to a perfectly normal state; and, invigorating the vital powers, excreted all foreign matters—the germs of diseases—by natural ways (perspiration and so) thereby makes man perfectly healthy in body and mind, and enables him to understand the proper guidance of Nature.

When this love becomes developed in man it makes him able to understand the real position of his own Self as well as of others surrounding him.

With the help of this developed love, man becomes fortunate in getting the God like company of the divine personages and is saved forever.

Without this love, man cannot live in the natural way, neither can he keep company of the fit person for his own welfare; he becomes often excited by the foreign matters taken into his system by mistakes in understanding the guidance of Nature, and in consequence suffers in body and mind. He can never get any peace whatever, and his life becomesa burden.

Hence the culture of this love, the heavenly gift, is the principal thing for the attainment of holy salvation; it is impossible for man to advance a step toward the same without it. This vide 112–4.

"I know thy works, and thy labor, and thy patience, and how thou canst not bear them which are evil: and thou hast tried them which say they are apostles, and are not, and hast found them liars.

"And hast borne and hast patience, and for my name's sake hast labored, and hast not fainted.

"Nevertheless I have somewhat against thee, because thou hast left thy first love."

श्रद्धासेवितसद्गुरोः स्वभावजोपदेशपालने वीर्यलाभः । ७ ।

सर्व एव गुरवः सन्तापहारकाः संशयच्छेदकाः शान्तिप्रदायकाः

सत् तत्संगः ब्रह्मवत् करणीयः, विपरीतमसत्

विषवद्वर्जनीयम् । ८ ।

As explained in the previous chapter, this creation is substantially nothing but mere idea-play of Nature on the only Real Substance, God, the Eternal Father, who is Guru—the Supreme—in this universe. All things of this creation are therefore no other substance than this Guru, the Supreme Father, God Himself, perceived in plurality by the manifold aspects of the play of Nature. vide *John* chap x,34, and *Psalm* LXXXII 6.

"Jesus answered them, Is it not written in your law, I said, Ye are gods?"

"I have said, Ye are gods; and all of you are children of the most High."

Out of this creation, the object that relieves us of our miseries and doubts and administers peace to us, whether animate or inanimate, and however insignificant the same may be, is entitled to our utmost respect.

Even if it be regarded by others as an object of vilest contempt, it should be accepted as *Sat* (Saviour) and its company as Godlike. That which produces opposite results, destroying our peace, throwing us into doubts, and creating our miseries, should be considered *Asat*, the bane of all good, and should be avoided as such. The Indian sages have a saying:

अप्सु देवो मनुष्याणां दिवि देवो मनीषिणाम् ।
काष्ठलोष्ट्रेषु मूर्खाणां युक्तस्यात्मनि देवता ।।

[Some consider the deities to exist in water (i.e., natural elements) while the learned consider them to exist in heaven (astral world); the unwise seek them in wood and stones (i.e., in images or symbols), but the Yogi realizes God in the sanctuary of his own Self.]

To attain salvation men choose as their Saviour the objects that they can comprehend according to their own stage of evolution.

Thus, in general, people think that illness is a dire calamity; and as water, when properly administered, tends to remove illness, ignorant men may choose for their Divinity water itself.

Philosophers, being able to comprehend the internal electrical Light that shines within them, find their heart's love flowing energetically toward the Light that relieves them of all causes of excitation, cools down their system to a normal state, and, invigorating their vital powers, makes them perfectly healthy, both in body and in mind. They then accept this Light as their Divinity or Saviour.

Ignorant people in their blind faith would accept a piece of wood or stone as their Saviour or Divinity in the external creation, for which their heart's natural love will develop till by its energetic tendency it will relieve them of all exciting causes, cool their system down to a normal state, and invigorate their vital powers.

The adepts, on the other hand, having full control over the whole material world, find their Divinity or Saviour in Self and not outside in the external world.

Regard the Guru with deep love. To keep company with the Guru is not only to be in his physical presence (as this is sometimes impossible), but mainly means to keep him in our hearts and to be one with him in principle and to attune ourselves with him.

This thought has been expressed by Lord Bacon: "A crowd is not a company, it is a mere gallery of faces." To keep company, therefore, with the Godlike object is to associate him with *Sraddha*, the heart's love intensified in the sense above explained, by keeping his appearance and attributes fully in mind, and by reflecting on the same and affectionately following his instructions, lamblike. See John 1:29.

"Behold the Lamb of God, which taketh away the sin of the world."

By so doing, when man becomes able to conceive the sublime status of his divine brothers, he may be fortunate in remaining in their company and in securing help from any one of them whom he may choose as his Spiritual Preceptor, *Sat-Guru*, the Saviour.

Thus, to resume, *Virya* or moral courage can be obtained by the culture of *Sraddha*, that is, by devoting one's natural love to his Preceptor, by being always in his company (in the internal sense already explained), and by following with affection his holy instructions as they are freely and spontaneously given.

तद्वीर्यं यमनियमानुष्ठानात् दृढभूमिः । ९ ।

अहिंसासत्यास्तेयब्रह्मचर्यापरिग्रहादयो यमः । १० ।

शौचसन्तोषसद्गुरुपदेशपालनादयः नियमः । ११ ।

Moral courage is strengthened by observance of *Yama* (morality or self-control) and *Niyama* (religious rules).

Yama comprises non injury to others, truthfulness, non stealing, continence, and non covetousness.

Niyama means purity of body and mind, contentment in all circumstances, and obedience (following the instructions of the guru).

Firmness of moral courage can be attained by the culture of *Yama,* the religious forbearances: abstention from cruelty, dishonesty, covetousness, unnatural living, and unnecessary possessions; and of *Niyama,* the religious observances: purity in body and mind—cleaning the body externally and internally from all foreign matters which, being fermented, create different sorts of diseases in the system, and clearing the mind from all prejudices and dogmas that make one narrow—contentment in all circumstances; and obedience to the holy precepts of the divine personages.

What is natural living? To understand what natural living is, it will be necessary to distinguish it from what is unnatural. Living depends upon the selection of (1) food, (2) dwelling, and (3) company. To live naturally, the lower animals can select these for themselves by the help of their instincts and the natural sentinels placed at the sensory entrances—the organs of sight, hearing, touch, smell, and taste.

With men in general, however, these organs are so much perverted by unnatural living from very infancy that little reliance can be placed on their judgments. To understand, therefore, what our natural needs are, we ought to depend upon observation, experiment, and reason.

What is natural food for man? First, to select our natural food, our observation should be directed to the formation of the organs that aid in digestion and nutrition, the teeth and digestive canal; to the natural tendency of the organs of sense which guide animals to their food; and to the nourishment of the young.

Observation of teeth. By observation of the teeth we find that in carnivorous animals the incisors are little developed, but the canines are of striking length, smooth and pointed, to seize the prey. The molars also are pointed; these points, however, do not meet, but fit closely side by side to separate the muscular fibers.

In the herbivorous animals the incisors are strikingly developed, the canines are stunted (though occasionally developed into weapons, as in elephants), the molars are broad-topped and furnished with enamel on the sides only.

In the frugivorous all the teeth are of nearly the same height; the canines are little projected, conical, and blunt (obviously not intended for seizing prey but for exertion of strength). The molars are broad-topped and furnished at the top with enamel folds to prevent waste caused by their side motion, but not pointed for chewing flesh.

In omnivorous animals such as bears, on the other hand, the incisors resemble those of the herbivorous, the canines are like those of the carnivorous, and the molars are both pointed and broad-topped to serve a twofold purpose.

Now if we observe the formation of the teeth in man we find that they do not resemble those of the carnivorous, neither do they resemble the teeth of the herbivorous or the omnivorous. They do resemble, exactly, those of the frugivorous animals. The reasonable inference, therefore, is that man is a frugivorous or fruit-eating animal.

Observation of the digestive canal. By observation of the digestive canal we find that the bowels of carnivorous animals are 3 to 5 times the length of their body, measuring from the mouth to the anus; and their stomach is almost spherical. The bowels of the herbivorous are 20 to 28 times the length of their body and their stomach is more extended and of compound build.

But the bowels of the frugivorous animals are 10 to 12 times the length of their body; their stomach is somewhat broader than that of the carnivorous and has a continuation in the duodenum serving the purpose of a second stomach.

This is exactly the formation we find in human beings, though Anatomy says that the human bowels are 3 to 5 times the length of man's body— making a mistake by measuring the body from the crown to the soles, instead of from mouth to anus. Thus we can again draw the inference that man is, in all probability, a frugivorous animal.

Observation of organs of sense. By observation of the natural tendency of the organs of sense—the guideposts for determining what is nutritious— by which all animals are directed to their food, we find that when the carnivorous animal finds prey, he becomes so much delighted that his eyes begin to sparkle; he boldly seizes the prey and greedily laps the jetting blood.

On the contrary, the herbivorous animal refuses even his natural food, leaving it untouched, if it is sprinkled with a little blood. His senses of smell and sight lead him to select grasses and other herbs for his food, which he tastes with delight. Similarly with the frugivorous animals, we find that their senses always direct them to fruits of the trees and field.

In men of all races we find that their senses of smell, sound, and sight never lead them to slaughter animals; on the contrary they cannot bear even the sight of such killings. Slaughterhouses are always recommended to be removed far from the towns; men often pass strict ordinances forbidding the uncovered transportation of flesh meats.

Can flesh then be considered the natural food of man, when both his eyes and his nose are so much against it, unless deceived by flavors of spices, salt, and sugar? On the other hand, how delightful do we find the fragrance of fruits, the very sight of which often makes the mouth water! It may also be noticed that various grains and roots possess an agreeable odor and taste, though faint, even when unprepared.

Thus again, we are led to infer from these observations that man was intended to be a frugivorous animal.

Observation of the nourishment of the young. By observation of the nourishment of the young we find that milk is undoubtedly the food of the newborn babe. Abundant milk is not supplied in the breasts of the mother if she does not take fruits, grains, and vegetables as her natural food.

Cause of disease. Hence from these observations the only conclusion that can reasonably be drawn is that various grains, fruits, roots, and—for beverage—milk, and pure water openly exposed to air and sun are decidedly the best natural food for man. These, being congenial to the system when taken according to the power of the digestive organs, well chewed and mixed with saliva, are always easily assimilated.

Other foods are unnatural to man and being uncongenial to the system are necessarily foreign to it; when they enter the stomach, they are not properly assimilated. Mixed with the blood, they accumulate in the excretory and other organs not properly adapted to them. When they cannot find their way out, they subside in tissue crevices by the law of gravitation; and, being fermented, produce diseases, mental and physical, and ultimately lead to premature death.

Children's development. Experiment also proves that the nonirritant diet natural to the vegetarian is, almost without exception, admirably suited to children's development, both physical and mental.

Their minds, understanding, will, the principal faculties, temper, and general disposition are also properly developed.

Natural living calms passions. We find that when extraordinary means such as excessive fasting, scourging, or monastic confinement are resorted to for the purpose of suppressing the sexual passions, these means seldom produce the desired effect.

Experiment shows, however, that man can easily overcome these passions, the archenemy of morality, by natural living on a nonirritant diet, above referred to; thereby men gain a calmness of mind which every psychologist knows is the most favorable to mental activity and to a clear understanding, as well as to a judicial way of thinking.

Sexual desire. Something more should be said here about the natural instinct of propagation, which is, next to the instinct of self-preservation, the strongest in the animal body. Sexual desire, like all other desires, has a normal and an abnormal or diseased state, the latter resulting only from the foreign matter accumulated by unnatural living as mentioned above.

In the sexual desire everyone has a very accurate thermometer to indicate the condition of his health. This desire is forced from its normal state by the irritation of nerves that results from the pressure of foreign matter accumulated in the system, which pressure is exerted on the sexual apparatus and is at first manifested by an increased sexual desire followed by a gradual decrease of potency.

This sexual desire in its normal state makes man quite free from all disturbing lusts, and operates on the organism (awaking a wish for appeasement) only infrequently. Here again experiment shows that this desire, like all other desires, is always normal in individuals who lead a natural life as mentioned.

The root of the tree of life. The sexual organ—the junction of important nerve extremities, particularly of the sympathetic and spinal nerves (the principal nerves of the abdomen) which, through their connection with the brain, are capable of enlivening the whole system—is in a sense the root of the tree of life. Man well-instructed in the proper use of sex can keep his body and mind in proper health and can live a pleasant life throughout.

The practical principles of sexual health are not taught because the public regards the subject as unclean and indecent. Thus blinded, mankind presumes to clothe Nature in a veil because she seems to them impure, forgetting that she is always clean and that everything impure and improper lies in man's ideas, and not in Nature herself.

It is clear therefore that man, not knowing the truth about the dangers of misuse of the sexual power, and being compelled to wrong practices by the nervous irritation resulting from unnatural living, suffers troublesome diseases in life and ultimately becomes a victim of premature death.

Dwelling place of man. Secondly, about our dwelling place.

We can easily understand, when we feel displeasure on entering a crowded room after breathing fresh air on a mountaintop or in an expanse of field or garden, that the atmosphere of the town or any crowded place is quite an unnatural dwelling place. The fresh atmosphere of the mountaintop, or of the field or garden, or of a dry place under trees covering a large plot of land and freely ventilated with fresh air is the proper dwelling place for man according to Nature.

The company we should keep. And thirdly, as to the company we should keep. Here also, if we listen to the dictates of our conscience and consult our natural liking, we will at once find that we favour those persons whose magnetism affects us harmoniously, who cool our system, internally invigorate our vitality, develop our natural love, and thus relieve us of our miseries and administer peace to us.

This is to say, we should be in the company of the *Sat* or Saviour and should avoid that of the *Asat,* as described before. By keeping the company of *Sat* (the Saviour) we are enabled to enjoy perfect health, physical and mental, and our life is prolonged.

If on the other hand we disobey the warning of Mother Nature, without listening to the dictates of our pure conscience, and keep the company of whatever has been designated as *Asat,* an opposite effect is produced and our health is impaired and our life shortened.

Necessity of natural living and purity. Thus natural living is helpful for the practice of *Yama,* the ascetic forbearances as explained earlier. Purity of mind and body being equally important in the practice of *Niyama,* the ascetic observances already explained, every attempt should be made to attain that purity.

ततः पाशक्षयः । १२ ।

घृणालज्जाभयशोकजुगुप्साजातिकुलमानाः पाशाष्टकम् । १३ ।

तदा चित्तस्य महत्त्वम् वीरत्वं वा । १४ ।

गार्हस्थ्याश्रमोपयोग्यासनप्राणायामप्रत्याहारसाधनेषु

योग्यता च । १५ ।

स्थिरसुखमासनम् । १६ ।

प्राणानां संयमः प्राणायामः । १७ ।

इन्द्रियाणामन्तर्मुखत्वं प्रत्याहारः । १८ ।

Hence bondage disappears.

The eight bondages or snares are hatred, shame, fear, grief, condemnation, race prejudice, pride of family, and smugness.

(Removal of the eight bondages) leads to magnanimity of heart.

Thus one becomes fit to practice *Asana, Pranayama,* and *Pratyahara;* and to enjoy the householder's life (by fulfilling all one's desires and so getting rid of them).

Asana means a steady and pleasant posture of the body.

Pranayama means control over *prana,* life force.

Pratyahara means withdrawal of the senses from external objects.

The eight mean-nesses of the heart. Firmness of moral courage, when attained, removes all the obstacles in the way of salvation. These obstacles are of eight sorts—hatred, shame, fear, grief, condemnation, race prejudice, pride of pedigree, and a narrow sense of respectability—which eight are the mean-nesses of the human heart.

Awakening magnanimity of the heart. By the removal of these eight obstacles, *Viratwam* or *Mahattwam* (magnanimity of the heart) comes in, and this makes man fit for the practice of *Asana* (remaining in steady and pleasant posture), *Pranayama* (control over *prana,* involuntary nerve electricities), and *Pratyahara* (changing the direction of the voluntary nerve currents inward). These practices enable man to satisfy his heart by enjoying the objects of the senses as intended for *Garhasthyasrama* (domestic) life.

Value of *Pranayama*. Man can put the voluntary nerves into action whenever he likes, and can give them rest when fatigued. When all of these voluntary nerves require rest he sleeps naturally, and by this sleep the voluntary nerves, being refreshed, can work again with full vigour. Man's involuntary nerves, however, irrespective of his will, are working continuously of themselves from his birth.

As he has no control over them, he cannot interfere with their action in the least.

When these nerves become fatigued they also want rest and naturally fall asleep. This sleep of the involuntary nerves is called *Mahanidra,* the great sleep, or death. When this takes place, the circulation, respiration, and other vital functions being stopped, the material body naturally begins to decay. After a while, when this great sleep *Mahanidra* is over, man awakes, with all his desires, and is reborn in a new physical body for the accomplishment of his various yearnings. In this way man binds himself to life and death and fails to achieve final salvation.

Control over death. But if man can control these involuntary nerves by the aforesaid *Pranayama,* he can stop the natural decay of the material body and put the involuntary nerves (of the heart, lungs, and other vital organs) to rest periodically, as he does with his voluntary nerves in sleep. After such rest by *Pranayama* the involuntary nerves become refreshed and work with newly replenished life.

As after sleep, when rest has been taken by the voluntary nerves, man requires no help to awaken naturally; so after death also, when man has enjoyed a full rest, he awakens naturally to life in a new body on earth.

If man can "die," that is, consciously put his entire nervous system, voluntary and involuntary, to rest each day by practice of *Pranayama,* his whole physical system works with great vigor.

Life and death come under the control of the yogi who perseveres in the practice of *Pranayama.* In that way he saves his body from the premature decay that overtakes most men, and can remain as long as he wishes in his present physical form, thus having time to work out his karma in one body and to fulfill (and so get rid of) all the various desires of his heart.

Finally purified, he is no longer required to come again into this world under the influence of *Maya,* Darkness, or to suffer the "second death." See I *Corinthians* (Bible) 15:31, and *Revelation* (Bible) 2:10, 11.

"I protest by our rejoicing which I have in Christ [consciousness], I die daily."—St. Paul. "Be thou faithful unto death, and I will give thee a crown of life....He that overcometh shall not be hurt of the second death."

Necessity of *Pratyahara.* Man enjoys a thing when he so desires. At the time of the enjoyment, however, if he directs his organs of sense, through which he enjoys, toward the object of his desire, he can never be satisfied, and his desires increase in double force.

On the contrary, if he can direct his organs of sense inward toward his Self, at that time he can satisfy his heart immediately.

So the practice of the aforesaid *Pratyahara,* the changing of the direction of the voluntary nerve currents inward, is a desirable way to fulfill his worldly desires. Man must reincarnate again and again until all his earthly longings are worked out and he is free from all desires.

Necessity of *Asana.* Man cannot feel or even think properly when his mind is not in a pleasant state; and the different parts of the human body are so harmoniously arranged that if even any minutest part of it be hurt a little, the whole system becomes disturbed. So to comprehend a thing, that is, to feel a thing by the heart clearly, the practice of the aforesaid *Asana,* the steady and pleasant posture, is necessary.

चित्तप्रसादे सति सर्वभावोदयः स्मृतिः । १९ ।

तदेवार्थमात्रनिर्भासं स्वरूपशून्यमिव समाधिः । २० ।

ततः संयमस्तस्मात् ब्रह्मप्रकाशकप्रणवशब्दानुभवः । २१ ।

तस्मिन्नात्मनो योगो भक्तियोगस्तदा दिव्यत्त्वम् । २२ ।

Smriti, true conception, leads to knowledge of all creation.

Samadhi, true concentration, enables one to abandon individuality for universality.

Hence arises *Samyama* ("restraint" or overcoming the egoistic self), by which one experiences the *Aum* vibration that reveals God.

Thus the soul (is baptized) in *Bhakti Yoga* (devotion). This is the state of Divinity.

Smriti, the true conception. Man, when expert in the above-mentioned practices, becomes able to conceive or feel all things of this creation by his heart. This true conception is called *Smriti.*

Samadhi, true concentration. Fixing attention firmly on any object thus conceived, when man becomes as much identified with it as if he were devoid of his individual nature, he attains the state of *Samadhi* or true concentration.

Pranava Sabda, the Word of God. When man directs all his organs of sense toward their common center, the sensorium or *Sushumnadwara,* the door of the internal world, he perceives his God-sent luminous body of *Radha* or John the Baptist, and hears the peculiar "knocking" sound, *Pranava Sabda,* the Word of God. See *John* (Bible) 1:6, 7, 23.

"There was a man sent from God, whose name was John.

"The same came for a witness, to bear witness of the Light, that all men through him might believe."

"I am the voice of one crying in the wilderness."

Samyama, the concentration of the self. Thus perceiving, man naturally believes in the existence of the true Spiritual Light, and, withdrawing his self from the outer world, concentrates himself on the sensorium.

This concentration of the self is called *Samyama.*

Bhakti Yoga or baptism, the second birth of man. By this *Samyama* or concentration of self on the sensorium, man becomes baptized or absorbed in the holy stream of the Divine Sound. This baptism is called *Bhakti Yoga.*

In this state man repents; that is, turning from this gross material creation of Darkness, *Maya,* he climbs back toward his Divinity, the Eternal Father, whence he had fallen, and passing through the sensorium, the door, enters into an internal sphere, *Bhuvarloka.* This entrance into the internal world is the second birth of man. In this state man becomes *Devata,* a divine being.

मूढविक्षिप्तक्षिप्तैकाग्रनिरुद्धाश्चित्तभेदास्ततो
जात्यन्तरपरिणामः । २३ ।

Translation same as following commentary.

Five states of human heart. There are five states of the human heart: dark, propelled, steady, devoted, and clean. By these different states of the heart man is classified, and his evolutionary status determined.

मूढचित्तस्य विपर्ययवृत्तिवशाद् जीवस्य शूद्रत्वम्, तदा ब्रह्मणः
कलामात्रेन्द्रियग्राह्यस्थूलविषयप्रकाशात् कलिः । २४ ।

In the dark state of the heart, man harbours misconceptions (about everything). This state is a result of *Avidya,* Ignorance, and produces a *Sudra* (a man of the lowest caste). He can grasp only ideas of the physical world. This state of mind is prevalent in Kali Yuga, the Dark Age of a cycle.

The dark heart. In the dark state of the heart man misconceives; he thinks that this gross material portion of the creation is the only real substance in existence, and that there is nothing besides. However, this is contrary to the truth, as has been explained before, and is nothing but the effect of Ignorance, *Avidya.*

Sudra or servant class. In this state man is called *Sudra,* or belonging to the servant class, because his natural duty then is to serve the higher class people in order to secure their company and thereby prepare his heart to attain a higher stage.

Kali Yuga, the dark cycle. This state of man is called *Kali;* and whenever in any solar system man generally remains in this state and is ordinarily deprived of the power of advancing beyond the same, the whole of that system is said to be in Kali Yuga, the dark cycle.

ब्रह्मणः प्रथमपादपूर्णत्वे द्वितीयसूक्ष्मविषयज्ञानाप्राप्तसन्धिकाले

चित्तस्य विक्षेपस्तदा प्रमाणवृत्तिवशात् क्षत्रियत्वम् । २५ ।

ततः सद्गुरुलाभो भक्तियोगश्च तदालोकान्तरगमनम् । २६ ।

Passing beyond the first stage in Brahma's plan, man strives for enlightenment and enters the natural *Kshatriya* (warrior) caste.

He is propelled (by evolutionary forces) to struggle (for truth). He seeks a guru and appreciates his divine counsel. Thus a *Kshatriya* becomes fit to dwell in the worlds of higher understanding.

The propelled heart. When man becomes a little enlightened he compares his experiences relating to the material creation, gathered in his wakeful state, with his experiences in dream, and understanding the latter to be merely ideas, begins to entertain doubts as to the substantial existence of the former.

His heart then becomes propelled to learn the real nature of the universe and, struggling to clear his doubts, seeks for evidence to determine what is truth.

Kshatriya, **the military class.** In this state man is called *Kshatriya,* or one of the military class; and to struggle in the manner aforesaid becomes his natural duty, by whose performance he may get an insight into the nature of creation and attain the real knowledge of it.

Sandhisthala—**the place between higher and lower.** This *Kshatriya* state of man is called *Sandhisthala,* the place between higher and lower.

In this state men, becoming anxious for real knowledge, need help of one another; hence mutual love, the principal necessity for gaining salvation, appears in the heart.

Motivated by the energetic tendency of this love, man affectionately keeps company with those who destroy troubles, clear doubts, and afford peace to him, and hence avoids whatever produces the contrary result; he also studies scientifically the scriptures of divine personages.

When man finds *Sat-Guru,* the Saviour.

In this way man becomes able to appreciate what true faith is, and understands the real position of the divine personages when he is fortunate in securing the Godlike company of some one of them who will kindly stand to him as his Spiritual Preceptor, *Sat- Guru,* or Saviour.

Following affectionately the holy precepts, he learns to concentrate his mind, directing his organs of sense to their common centre or sensorium, *Sushumnadwara,* the door of the internal sphere.

There he perceives the luminous body of John the Baptist, or *Radha,* and hears the holy Sound (Amen, *Aum*) like a stream or river; and being absorbed or baptized in it, begins to move back toward his Divinity, the Eternal Father, through the different *Lokas* or spheres of the creation.

भूर्भुवःस्वर्महर्जनस्तपः सत्यमिति सप्त लोकाः । २७ ।

The worlds or *Lokas* of creation are seven: *Bhu, Bhuvar, Swar, Mahar, Jana, Tapo,*and *Satya.*

(This earth, and the "earthy" stage of man's consciousness, are called *Bhuloka.*)

The Seven *Lokas.* In the way toward Divinity there are seven spheres or stages of creation, designated as *Swargas* or *Lokas* by the Oriental sages, as described in Chapter 1:13.

These are *Bhuloka,* the sphere of gross matters; *Bhuvarloka,* the sphere of fine matters or electric attributes; *Swarloka,* the sphere of magnetic poles and auras or electricities; *Maharloka,* the sphere of magnets, the atoms; *Janaloka,* the sphere of Spiritual Reflections, the Sons of God; *Tapoloka,* the sphere of the Holy Ghost, the Universal Spirit; and *Satyaloka,* the sphere of God, the Eternal Substance, *Sat.*

Of these seven planes, the first three (*Bhuloka, Bhuvarloka,* and *Swarloka*) comprise the material creation, the kingdom of Darkness, *Maya;* and the last three (*Janaloka, Tapoloka,* and *Satyaloka*) comprise the spiritual creation, the kingdom of Light. *Maharloka* or the sphere of Atom, being in the midst, is said to be the "door" communicating between these two—the material and spiritual creation—and is called *Dasamadwara,* the tenth door, or *Brahmarandhra,* the way to Divinity.

भुवर्लोके ब्रह्मणः द्वितीयपादसूक्ष्मान्तर्जगत्प्रकाशाद् द्वापरः, जीवस्य द्विजत्त्वञ्च, तदा चित्तस्य क्षिप्तत्वात्तस्य वृत्तिर्विकल्पः । २८ ।

Entering *Bhuvarloka* ("air" or "the world of becoming") man becomes a *Dvija* or "twice-born."

He comprehends the second portion of material creation—that of finer, subtler forces. This state of mind is prevalent in Dwapara Yuga.

Dvija or twice-born. When man, being baptized, begins to repent and move back toward the Eternal Father and, withdrawing his self from the gross material world, *Bhuloka,* enters into the world of fine matter, *Bhuvarloka,* he is said to belong to the *Dvija* or twice-born class.

In this state he comprehends his internal electricities, the second fine material portion of the creation; and understands that the existence of the external is substantially nothing but mere coalescence or union of his fine internal objects of sense (the negative attributes of electricities) with his five organs of sense (the positive attributes) through his five organs of action (the neutralizing attributes of the same), caused by the operation of his mind and conscience (consciousness).

The steady heart. This state of man is *Dwapara;* and when this becomes the general state of human beings naturally in any solar system, the whole of that system is said to be in Dwapara Yuga. In this *Dwapara* state the heart becomes steady.

If man continues in the baptized state, remaining immersed in the holy stream, he gradually comes to a pleasant state wherein his heart wholly abandons the ideas of the external world and becomes devoted to the internal one.

स्वर्गे चित्तस्यैकाग्रतया वृत्तिः स्मृतिस्ततः

ब्रह्मणस्तृतीयपादजगत्कारणप्रकृतिज्ञानवशात्

त्रेता, तदा विप्रत्वं जीवस्य । २९ ।

In *Swarloka* ("heaven") man is fit to understand the mysteries of *Chitta,* the magnetic third portion of material creation. He becomes a *Vipra* (nearly perfect being). This state of mind is prevalent in Treta Yuga.

29- In this devoted state man, withdrawing his self from bhuploka, the world of electric attributes, comes to *Swarloka,* the world of magnetic attributes, the electricities and poles; when he becomes able to comprehend *Chitta,* Heart, the magnetic third portion of creation.

This *Chitta,* as explained in Chapter 1, being the spiritualized Atom, *Avidya* or Ignorance, a part of Darkness, *Maya.* Man, comprehending this *Chitta,* becomes able to understand the whole of Darkness, *Maya* itself, of which *it* is a part, as well as its entire creation. Man is then said to belong to the *Bipra,* or perfect, class. This state of human beings is called *Treta;* when this becomes the general state of the higher beings naturally in any solar system, the whole of that system is said to be in Treta Yuga.

महर्लोके चित्तस्य निरुद्धत्वात्तस्य वृत्तिर्निद्रा

ततः सर्वविकाराभावे ब्रह्मवत् स्वात्मानुभवात्

ब्रह्मणत्वन्तदाब्रह्मणस्तुरीयांशसत्पदार्थप्रकाशात् सत्यम् । ३० ।

Man repenting (creeping back) further lifts up his self to *Maharloka,* the region of magnet; then all the developments of Ignorance being withdrawn, the heart comes to a clean state, void of all external ideas.

Then man becomes able to comprehend the Spiritual Light, Brahma, the Real Substance in the universe, which is the last and everlasting spiritual portion in creation. In this stage man is called *Brahmana* or spiritual class. This stage of the human being is called *Satya,* and when this becomes the general state of higher beings naturally in any solar system, the whole of that system is said to be in Satya Yuga.

तदपि संन्यासान् मायातीतजनलोकस्थे मुक्तसंन्यासी

ततः चैतन्यप्रकटिततपोलोके आत्मनोऽर्पणात् सत्यलोकस्थे

कैवल्यम् । ३१-३२ ।

31-32. In this way, when the heart becomes Perfectly purified it does no more reflects but receive Spiritual Light, the Son of God; and thus being consecrated or anointed by the Spirit it becomes Christ, the Saviour, the only way through which man, being again baptized or absorbed in Spirit, come above the creation of Darkness and enter into *Janaloka,* the Kingdom of God; that is, the creation of Light. In this state man is called *Jivanmukta Sannyasi,* like Lord Jesus of Nazareth. Vide *John IIT* 5 XIV 6.

"Verily, verily, I say unto thee, Except a man be born of water and of the Spirit, he cannot enter into the kingdom of God."

"Jesus saith unto him, I am the way, the truth, and the life: no man cometh unto the Father, but by me."

In this state man comprehends himself as nothing but a mere ephemeral idea resting on a fragment of the universal Holy Spirit of God, the Eternal Father, and understanding the real worship, he sacrifices his self there at this Holy Spirit, the altar of God; that is, abandoning the vain idea of his separate existence, becomes "dead" or dissolved in the universal Holy Spirit; and thus come to *Tapoloka,* the region of the Holy Ghost.

In this manner, being one and the same with the universal Holy Spirit of God, man becomes unified with the Eternal Father Himself, and so comes to *Satyaloka,* when he comprehends that all this creation is substantially nothing but a mere idea-play of his own nature, and there nothing in the universe besides his own Self. This state of unification is called *Kaibalya,* the Sole Self. vide Rev .XIV .13 and john XVI28.

"Blessed are the dead which die in the Lord from henceforth."

"I came forth from the Father; and am come into the world: again, I leave the world, and go to the Father."

CHAPTER 4

THE REVELATION

विभूतिः

सहजद्रव्यतपोमन्त्रैः देहत्रयशुद्धिस्ततः सिद्धिः । १ ।

सद्‌गुरुकृपया सा लभ्या । २ ।

सहजद्रव्येण स्थूलस्य तपसा सूक्ष्मस्य मन्त्रेण

कारणदेहचित्तस्य च शुद्धिः । ३ ।

1-3. Adeptship is attainable by the purification of the body in all respects. Purification of the material body can be effected by things generated along with it by Nature; that of the electric body by patience in all circumstances; and that of the magnetic body (*chitta*) by regulation of the breath, which is called *mantra,* (मनः त्रायत इति मन्त्रः) the purifier of the mind.

The process how purifications can be effected may be learnt at the feet of the divine personages who witness Light and bear testimony of Christ.

साधनप्रभावेण प्रणवशब्दाविर्भावस्तदेव मन्त्रचैतन्यम् । ४ ।

देशभेदे तस्य भेदात् मन्त्रभेदः साधकेषु । ५ ।

4-5. By culture of regulation of the breath as directed by the Spiritual Preceptor (*Sat-Guru*), the holy Word (प्रणव, शब्द) *Pranava* or *Sabda* appears by itself or becomes audible.

When this *holy* (Word, *Pranava*) or sabda appears mantra, the breath becomes regulated and checks the decay of the material body.

This *Pranava* appears in different forms at the different stages of advancement, according to the purification of the heart (*Chitta*).

श्रद्धायुक्तस्य सद्गुरुलाभस्ततः प्रवृत्तिस्तदैव

प्रवर्त्तकावस्था जीवस्य । ६ ।

6. It has already been explained what *Sat-Guru* is and how to keep the company thereof. Man, when endowed with the heavenly gift of pure love, naturally becomes disposed to avoid the company of what is *Asat* and to keep the company of what has been described as *Sat*.

By affectionately keeping the company of *Sat* he may be fortunate enough to please one who may kindly stand to him as his *Sat-Guru* a Spiritual Preceptor.

By keeping his Godlike company there grows an inclination, *Prabritti,* in his heart to save himself from the creation of darkness, *Maya,* and he becomes *Prabartaka,* an initiate in the practices of *Yama* and *Niyama,* the ascetic forbearances and observances necessary to obtain salvation.

यमनियमसाधनेन पशुत्वनाशस्ततः वीरत्वमासनादिसाधने

योग्यता च तदैव साधकावस्था प्रवर्त्तकस्य । ७ ।

7. It may be remembered that by the culture of *Yama* and *Niyama,* the mean-nesses vanish from the heart and magnanimity comes in.

It is at this stage that man becomes fit for the practice of ascetic posture etc. The processes pointed out by his *Sat-Guru* to attain salvation; when he continues to practice the processes so pointed out to him by his Sad Guru to attain salvation and hen he continues to practice the processes so pointed out to him . he becomes a *Sadhaka* or disciple.

ततः भावोदयात् दिव्यत्चं तस्मिन् समाहिते देववाणी

प्रणवानुभवस्तदैव सिद्धावस्था साधकस्य । ८ ।

8. On reference to Chapter 3 it will be found how a disciple, while passing through the different stages, becomes able to conceive the different objects of creation in his heart; and how he gradually advances to the states of meditation; and ultimately, by concentrating his attention to the sensorium, he perceives the peculiar sound, *Pranava* or *Sabda,* the holy Word, when the heart becomes divine and the Ego, *Ahamkara,* or son of man becomes merged or baptized in the stream thereof, and the disciple becomes *Siddha,* an adept, a divine personage.

तत्संयमात् सप्तपातालदर्शनम् ऋषिसप्तकस्य चाविर्भावः । ९ ।

In the state of Baptisation (*Bhakti Yoga, Surat Sabda Yoga,*) man repents and withdraws his self from the external world of gross matters, *Bhuloka,* and enters into the internal one of fine matter, the *Bhubarloka ;*

Where he perceives the manifestation of Spirit, the true Light, like seven stars in seven centers or conspicuous places, which have been compared to seven golden candlesticks. These stars, being the manifestation of true Light, the Spirit, are called angels or *rishis,* which appear one after another in the right hand of the son of man; that is, in his right way to Divinity.

The seven golden candlesticks are called chuches the seven golden conspicuous places in the body, known as brain, the *sahasrara;* medulla oblongata, the *ajna chakra;* and five spinal centers—cervical, *bishuddha;* dorsal, *anahata;* lumbar, *manipura;* sacral, *swadhishthana;* and coccygeal, *muladhara,* where the Spirit becomes manifested. Through these seven centers or churches, Ego the son of Man passes toward the Divinity; Vide Rev. Ch. I : 12,13,16 and Ch. II.

"And being turned, I saw seven golden candlesticks; and in the midst of the seven candlesticks one like unto the son of man....And he had in his right hand seven stars."

"The mystery of the seven stars which thou sawest in my right hand, and the seven golden candlesticks. The seven stars are the angels of the seven churches; and the seven candlesticks which thou sawest are the seven churches."

"These things saith he that holdeth the seven stars in his right hand, who walketh in the midst of the seven golden candlesticks."

9. In this state of baptism (*Bhakti Yoga* or *Surat Sabda Yoga*) as Ego, *Surat,* the son of man, gradually passing through the seven places mentioned, acquires the knowledge thereof; and when thus completes the journey through the whole of these regions he understands the true nature of the universe. Withdrawing his self from *Bhubarloka,* the fine material creation, and enters into *Swarloka,* the source of all matters, fine and gross.

There he perceives his luminous astral form around his Heart, Atom, the throne of Spirit the Creator, provided with five electricities and two poles, Mind and Intelligence, of seven different colors as in rainbows.

In this sphere of electricities, mind and intelligence, the source of all objects of senses and of organs for their enjoyment, man becomes perfectly satisfied with being in possession of all objects of his desires, and acquires a complete knowledge thereof. Hence the astral form with its electricities and poles, the seven seals. parts thereof has been described as a sealed casket of knowledge, a book with seven seals. Vide Rev. Ch. V.11 V, 3.

"And there was a rainbow round about the throne."

"And I saw in the right hand of him that sat on the throne a book written within and on the back side, sealed with seven seals."

तदा ज्ञानशक्तियोगक्रमात्

सप्तस्वर्गाधिकारस्ततश्चतुर्मनूनामाविर्भावः । १० ।

10. Passing through this *Swarloka,* the son of man comes to *Maharloka,* the place of magnet , of which the ideas of manifestation Time, Space, and particle (Atom) are the four component parts.

As mentioned in Chapter 1, this *Maharloka* represents *Avidya,* Ignorance, which produces the idea of separate existence of self and is the source of Ego, the son of man.

Thus man (मानव, *manava*), being the offspring of Ignorance, and Ignorance being represented by the four ideas aforesaid, these ideas are called the four *manus* (मनु + ष्ण = मानव), the origins or sources of man.

ततः भूतजयादणिमाद्यैश्वर्यस्याविर्भावः । ११ ।

11. The Maharloka, the place of Magnet as explained before, is the *Brahmarandhra* or *Dasamadwara,* the door between two creations, material and spiritual. When Ego, the son of man, comes to the the same, he comprehends the Spiritual Light and becomes baptized therein.

And passing through this door he comes above the ideal creation of Darkness, *Maya,* and entering into the spiritual world, receives the true Light and becomes the Son of God.

Thus man, being the Son of God, overcomes all bondage of Darkness, *Maya,* and becomes possessed of all *aiswaryas,* the ascetic majesties. These *aiswaryas* are of eight sorts:

Anima, the power of making one's body or anything else as small as he likes, even as tiny as an atom, *anu.*

Mahima, the power of magnifying or making one's body or anything else *mahat,* as large as he likes.

Laghima, the power of making one's body or anything else *laghu,* as light as he likes.

Garima, the power of making one's body or anything else *guru,* asheavy as he likes.

Prapti, the power of *apti,* obtaining anything he likes.

Basitwa, the power of *basha,* bringing anything under control.

Prakamya, the power of satisfying all desires, *kama,* by irresistible willforce.

Isitwa, the power of becoming isha Lord over everything Vide John XIV 12.

"Verily, verily, I say unto you, he that believeth on me, the works that I do shall he do also; and greater works than these shall he do; because I go unto my Father."

ततः सृष्टिस्थितिप्रलयज्ञानात् सर्वनिवृत्तिः ।

तदा मायातिक्रमे आत्मनः परमात्मनि दर्शनात् कैवल्यम् । १२ ।

Thus man, being possessed of, *aiswaryas* the ascetic majesties aforesaid, fully comprehends the Eternal Spirit, the Father, the only Real Substance, as Unit, the Perfect Whole, and his Self as nothing but a mere idea resting on a fragment of the Spiritual Light thereof. Man, thus comprehending, abandons altogether the vain idea of the separate existence of his own Self and becomes unified with Him, the Eternal Spirit, God the Father. This unification with God is *Kaibalya*, the ultimate object of this treatise Vide. Rev. III 21.

"To him that overcometh will I grant to sit with me in my throne, even as I also overcame, and am set down with my Father in his throne."

CONCLUSION

"Love rules the court, the camp, the grove, The men below
and saints above; For love is heaven and heaven is love."

The power of love has been beautifully described by the poet in the stanza quoted above. It has been clearly demonstrated in the foregoing pages that "Love is God," not merely as the noblest sentiment of a poet but an aphorism containing an eternal truth. To whatever religious creed a man may belong and whatever may his position in society, if he properly cultivates this ruling principle naturally implanted in his heart, he is sure to be on the right path to save himself from his creation of Darkness, *Maya*.

It has been shown in the foregoing pages how love may be cultivated, how by its culture it attains development, and when developed, how through this only, man may find his Spiritual Preceptor, through whose favor again he becomes baptized in the holy stream, and sacrifices his Self before the altar of God, and become unified with the Eternal Father forever and ever.

This little volume is therefore concluded with an earnest exhortation to the reader that they may never forget that life is always unsafe and unstable like a drop of water on a lotus leaf and that the company of a Divine personage for a moment can save it like Noahs ark in the flood as has been very poetically described by the Indian sage Shankaracharyya in the following Slokas -

"नलिनीदलगतजलमतितरलं तद्वज्जीवनमतिशयचपलम् ।
क्षणमिह सज्जनसंगतिरेका भवति भवार्णवतरणे नौका ॥"

Printed by P. L. Dey
The Kidderpore Press,
21, Cir. Garden Reach Road, Kidderpore, Calcutta.

Swami Sri Yukteshwarji's remarkable encounter with Mahavatar Babaji, the Guru of Lahiri Mahasaya, in 1894.

<u>Mentioned in Autobiography of a Yogi (1946 Original Edition - Which is in public domain.)</u>

Sri Yukteswar told the story of that memorable meeting as follows:

"Welcome, Swamiji," Babaji said affectionately.

"Sir," I replied emphatically, "I am *not* a swami."

"Those on whom I am divinely directed to bestow the title of *swami* never cast it off."

The saint addressed me simply, but deep conviction of truth rang in his words; I was instantly engulfed in a wave of spiritual blessing. Smiling at my sudden elevation into the ancient monastic order, I bowed at the feet of the obviously great and angelic being in human form who had thus honoured me....

"I saw that you are interested in the West, as well as in the East." Babaji's face beamed with approval. "I felt the pangs of your heart, broad enough for all men. That is why I summoned you here.

"East and West must establish a golden middle path of activity and spirituality combined," he continued.

"India has much to learn from the West in material development; in return, India can teach the universal methods by which the West will be able to base its religious beliefs on the unshakable foundations of yogic science."

"You, Swamiji, have a part to play in the coming harmonious exchange between Orient and Occident. Some years hence I shall send you a disciple whom you can train for yoga dissemination in the West. The vibrations there of many spiritually seeking souls come flood-like to me. I perceive potential saints in America and Europe, waiting to be awakened...."

"At my request, Swamiji," the great master said, "will you not write a short book on the underlying harmony between Christian and Hindu scriptures? Their basic unity is now obscured by men's sectarian differences. Show by parallel references that the inspired sons of God have spoken the same truths."

Returning to Serampore, Sri Yukteswarji began his literary efforts. "In the quiet of night I busied myself over a comparison of the Bible and the scriptures of *Sanatana Dharma,*" he later recounted.

"Quoting the words of the blessed Lord Jesus, I showed that his teachings are in essence one with the revelations of the Vedas. Through the grace of my *Param Guru,* my book, *<u>The Holy Science,</u>* <u>was finished in a short time.</u>"

The Holy Science
1920 Original Edition

Editions

As one reads in the foreword of the 1920 Edition, Sri Yukteswar published the chapters of *The Holy Science* first in various segments in his *Sadhusambad* journal. This is how the journals looked like:

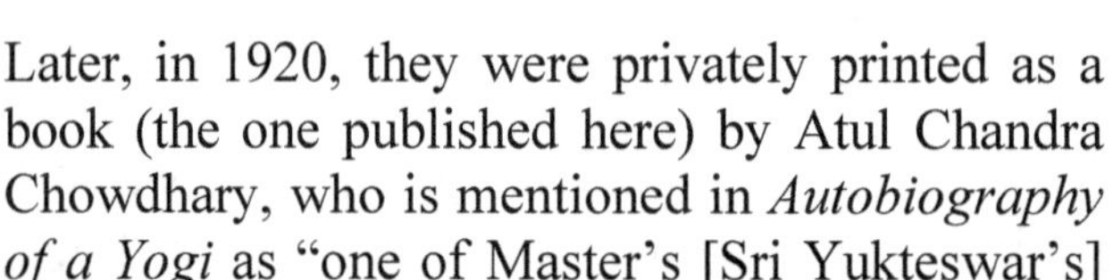

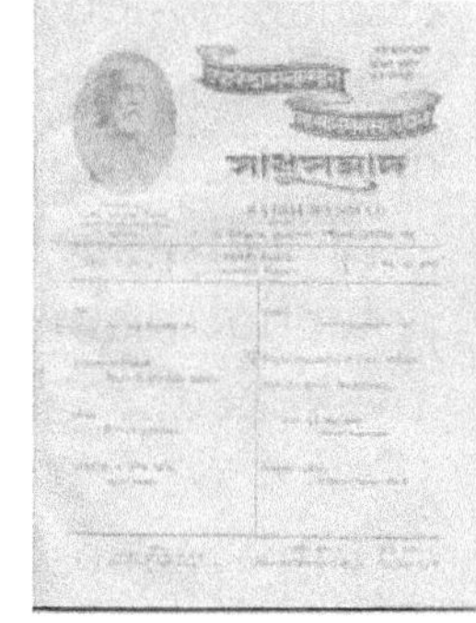

Later, in 1920, they were privately printed as a book (the one published here) by Atul Chandra Chowdhary, who is mentioned in *Autobiography of a Yogi* as "one of Master's [Sri Yukteswar's] chelas in Calcutta." He was the Secretary of Sri Yukteswar's organization *Sadhusabha*. The book was called *Kaivalya Darsanam*, translated as "Exposition of Final Truth."

Still later, in 1949, *The Holy Science* was printed by SRF, slightly edited (Bengali terms were now presented in Sanskrit, for example *kal* became *kala* etc.; grammar was corrected; the introduction was modified). Yogananda wrote a foreword for that edition, in which he mentions that Sri Yukteswar expounds the *Sankhya* philosophy along with quotes from *Revelation*. (*Sankhya* is one of the six *darshanas*, Vedic philosophies). It is interesting that Yogananda focuses on these two, as Sri Yukteswar discusses not only India's *Sankhya* (as we will see), nor only *Revelation* from the Bible: there are numerous quotes from the New Testament, words of Jesus. It might be, however, that *Sankhya* and *Revelation* are the most striking features in the book.

1

For the 1962 edition the Sanskrit *sutras* were translated into English, an obvious necessity for Western readers.

This is how the 1974 Edition looked like:

A Thought About the Yugas
Often the Sri Yukteswar's Yuga system is placed at the center of discussion where *The Holy Science* is concerned. In fact however, this topic is only a part of his introduction. His Yuga explanations are fascinating and revolutionary, but the real essence and challenge of his book remains the science of God-Oneness, and the parallel teachings in Eastern and Western scriptures.

The Sanskrit *Sutras*
A question sometimes asked is: are the Sanskrit *Sutras* in *The Holy Science* direct quotes from ancient scriptures, or were they composed by Sri Yukteswar?

In *Autobiography of a Yogi* Sri Yukteswar explains his intention concerning the book: "Quoting the words of the blessed Lord Jesus, I showed that his teachings were in essence one with the revelations of the *Vedas*." In other words, he states that his *Sutras* are from the Vedas (including all other Indian scriptures which are "offspring" of the Vedas).

On the other hand Swami Satyananda writes in his book *Swami*

2

Sri Yuktesvar Giri Maharaj- A Biography: "He began to <u>create</u> Sanskrit *Sutras* based on the unifying conclusions of eastern philosophy and sadhana, and alongside these *Sutras*, he wrote down the...."

Probably, then, Sri Yukteswar composed these *Sutras*, which represented essential thoughts from the sacred Indian Scriptures.

SRF explains in a *Note to the Seventh Edition*, 1972: "...of all the Sanskrit Sutras <u>set down</u> by Swami Sri Yukteswar..... ", "of each Sutra (precept <u>summarizing</u> Vedic teaching)...."

J.C. Bhattacharya who published a biography on Sri Yukteswar states similarly: "The conclusions of the Hindu Scriptures he embodied in Sanskrit Sutras (dictums) composed by himself."

Union of Six Indian Philosophies (*darshanas*)

The very first words of Swami Sri Yukteswar, written in Sanskrit, state a fascinating fact: his book *The Holy Science* expounds the six *darshanas*: the six Vedic philosophies (Sankhya, Yoga, Vendanta, Nyaya, Mimansa, Vaisesika). These first Sanskrit words were translated into English in 1962, but insufficiently (maybe because the six *darshanas* would have been too much to digest for readers at that time, when yoga was still very new in the West). Readers may look up that Introduction in modern versions of *The Holy Science*, which begins with the words:
"[This *Kaivalya Darsanam*, (exposition of Final Truth) has been written by Priya Nath Swami...."

An important part is missing in that English translation. Swami Satyananda in his book, *Swami Sri Yuktesvar Giri Maharaj- A Biography* offers that same Sanskrit text in a transliterated version, followed by the complete English translation:

3

"In the 194 year of the Dvapara Yuga, in the Prayag, in order to *analyze the teaching of the six systems of philosophy*, having obtained the permission of the Lord Parama-Guru, Priyanatha Swami of the family of Karar, son of Kadambini and Kshetranath, presents this 'Darsha-Kaivalya' for the well-fare of the world."

Indeed in *The Holy Science* one finds typical elements of the six philosophies (*darshana*). Three of them, *Sankhhya, Yoga, Vedanta*, are listed below. Professional scholars and *pundits* may complete this insufficient list. Sri Yukteswar in his *The Holy Science* unites these schools of thought, which are usually considered rivals, teaching contrasting and opposing philosophies. Here are at least three of the six *darshanas (Sankhya, Yoga, Vedanta)*, and how Sri Yukteswar imbedded them in *The Holy Science:*

Sankhya

The first chapter in *The Holy Science* is almost pure *Shankhya*. Sri Yukteswar describes the cosmos in *Shankhya* terms, explaining its 24 basic principles of creation (Sutra I;12). They are:
- **AUM** (in Shankya called *Moola Prakriti*)
- **Mahat** (Sri Yukteswar in Sutra I,6 writes that *Mahat* is the same as *chitta*); in Shankhya *mahat* brings forth *buddhi. Mahat* or *chitta* contains not only *buddhi*, but also *manas* and *ahankara.*
- **Manas** (sensory mind; *manas* and *buddhi* polarize *chitta*: *buddhi* pulling it to God, *manas* outward)
- **Ahankara** (ego; as said, it too comes out of *chitta*)
- **5 Jnanendriyas** (sense organs of perception: smell, taste, sight, touch, hearing)
- **5 Karmendrias** (organs of action: excretion, generation/procreation, motion, manual skill, speech)

4

- **5 Tanmatras** (usually called "subtle elements," which Sri Yukteswar describes as *objects* of the senses of smell, taste, sight, touch, sound)
- **5 Mahabhutas** (5 elements: earth, water, fire, air, ether)

Sankhya is usually understood to be a atheistic philosophy, which Sri Yukteswar corrects in his exposition. His first three Sutras explain that everything is and comes from God (Parambrahma). In fact, in the *Autobiography of a Yogi* he says: "Because of one *Sankhya* aphorism, *Iswar-ashidha,–* 'A Lord of Creation cannot be deduced' or 'God is not proved,' many scholars call the whole philosophy atheistical. The verse is not nihilistic," Sri Yukteswar explained. "It merely signifies that to the unenlightened man, dependent on his senses for all final judgments, proof of God must remain unknown and therefore non-existent. True *Sankhya* followers, with unshakable insight born of meditation, understand that the Lord is both existent and knowable."

Yoga (the Yoga Sutras)

Sri Yukteswar in *The Holy Science* uses famous terms of Patanjali's Yoga Sutras, offering his exposition of yama, niyama (III;9-11), asana, pranayama, pratyahara (III,12-18). He uses Patanjali's term *Samyama* (III;19-22), which is *dharana, dhyana, samadhi* combined. Along with it he refers to *smriti* (divine memory), a typical concept used by Patanjali.

The important and revolutionary concept in *The Holy Science* is that *chitta* is explained as "heart," (I;6) a teaching which later Yogananda taught as well. Usually when talking about Patanjali's famous definition *"yogas chitta vritti nirodha,"* *chitta* is explained variously as memory, consciousness, subconsciousness, mind-stuff, thought, mind. Yogananda, following Sri Yukteswar, taught *chitta* to be "feeling" or "primordial feeling."

5

In truth, if one studies it carefully, everything in *The Holy Science* revolves around the Heart (*chitta*). Sri Yukteswar concludes his book therefore: "It has been clearly demonstrated in the foregoing pages that "God is Love," not only as the noblest sentiment of a poet, but as an aphorism of eternal truth."

The oldest extant commentary of the Yoga Sutras is *Yoga Bhasya*, by Vyasa. In it (III,45) are described the "Ashta-siddhi," the eight powers which Sri Yukteswar also describes in *The Holy Science* (Sutra IV;11).

Sri Yukteswar also includes the teaching from the same Scripture *Yoga Bhasya* (III,26), that the universe is structured in 14 spheres or worlds: the seven *lokas* (usually called "upper worlds") and the seven *patalas* ("lower worlds"). Sri Yukteswar explains (I,13) that the *patalas* are not as commonly understood "worlds under the earth" (netherworlds), but the chakras. In them reside the scriptural *sapta-rishis*, the seven rishis, who are usually taught to be in patriarchs of the world.

Vedanta

All *Upanishads* are Vendanta. The ancient *Taittiriya Upanishad* (II,7) explains the 5 Koshas (Pancha Kosha), a concept which Sri Yukteswar picks up in his *The Holy Science* (I,14).

Sri Yukteswar also discusses the three bodies (causal, astral, material), a Vedanta teaching.

The very first three Sutras of *The Holy Science* are pure Vedanta: how *Parambrahma* (God) is everything, causes everything; later (I,15,16) Sri Yukteswar explains that the created world is *maya*, illusion, unreal; and that the mystical

6

way back to the realization of Brahman as the only Reality is through AUM: all this is pure *Vedanta*.

The very last Sutra in *The Holy Science* is vedantic too: "Beholding the self in the Supreme Self, man gains eternal freedom." This could be a direct sentence by Adi Shankaracharya, one of the foremost expounders of Vedanta (Advaita Vedanta). Shankaracharya wrote: "Brahman is the only truth, the spatio-temporal world is an illusion, and there is ultimately no difference between Brahman and individual self."

CONCLUSION

We might conclude that Sri Yukteswar was a great believer in harmony, in union. He tried, at Mahavatar Babaji's behest, to reconcile the six *darshanas* amongst themselves and with the Biblical teachings. He was also a yogi who believed in the harmonious union between science and religion: a teaching which Yogananda later expanded on. May this harmony and unity spread everywhere on our planet, as *Dwapara Yuga* manifests itself ever more purely.

7

Sri Yukteswarji's Cosmology (SANKHYA)
in The Holy Science

All quotes are from the first chapter, from the 1920 original edition.

Some Sanskrit terms have been adjusted: for example kal→ kala.

Sutra 1,1

The Eternal Father God, Swami Parambrahma, is the only Real Substance, SAT in unit, and is all in all in the universe.

SAT

Sutra 1.2

The Almighty Force, Shakti, or in other words the Eternal Joy, Ananda, which produces the world; and the Omniscient Feeling, Chit, which makes this world conscious, demonstrate the Nature, Prakriti, of God the Father

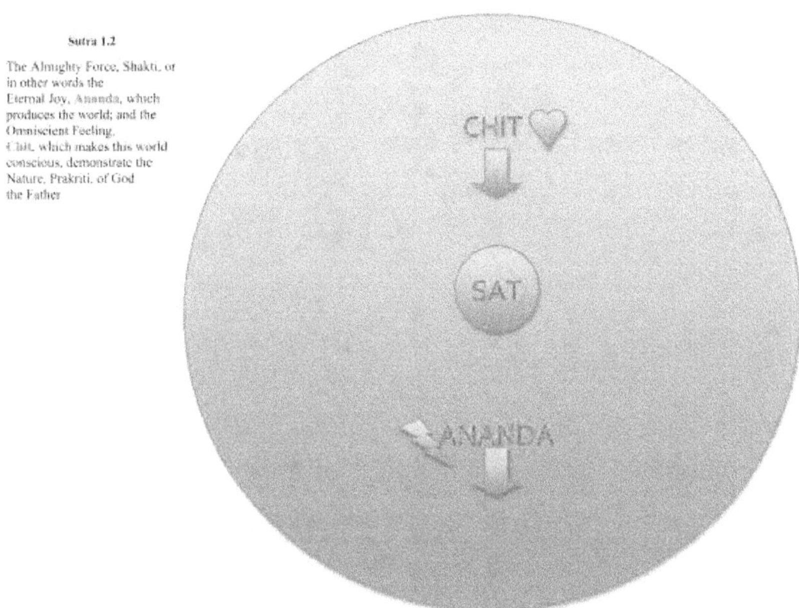

Sutra 1.2

The Almighty Force, Shakti, or in other words the Eternal Joy, Ananda, which produces the world; and the Omniscient Feeling, Chit, which makes this world conscious, demonstrate the Nature, Prakriti, of God the Father.

CHIT SAT ANANDA

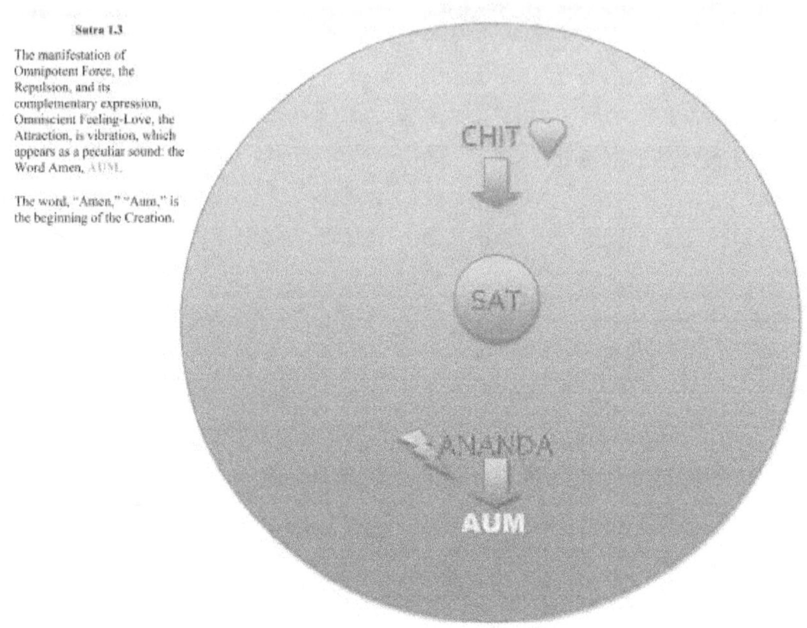

Sutra 1.3

The manifestation of Omnipotent Force, the Repulsion, and its complementary expression, Omniscient Feeling-Love, the Attraction, is vibration, which appears as a peculiar sound: the Word Amen, AUM.

The word, "Amen," "Aum," is the beginning of the Creation.

CHIT SAT ANANDA AUM

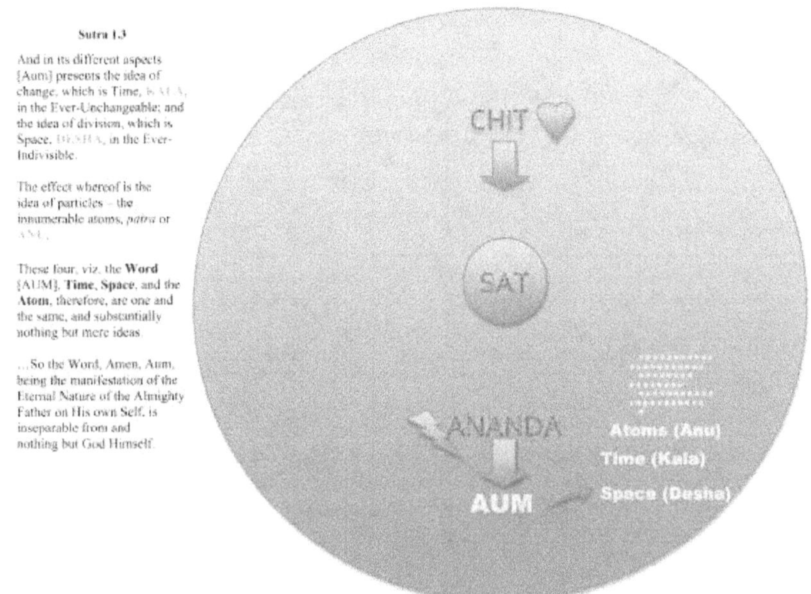

Sutra 1.3

And in its different aspects [Aum] presents the idea of change, which is Time, KALA, in the Ever-Unchangeable; and the idea of division, which is Space, DESHA, in the Ever- Indivisible.

The effect whereof is the idea of particles-the innumerable atoms, patra or ANU.

These four, viz. the Word [AUM], Time, Space, and the Atom, therefore, are one and the same, and substantially nothing but mere ideas.

...So the Word, Amen, Aum, being the manifestation of the Eternal Nature of the Almighty Father on His own Self, is inseparable from and nothing but God Himself.

CHIT SAT ANANDA : Atoms (Anu) Time (Kala) Space (Desha)

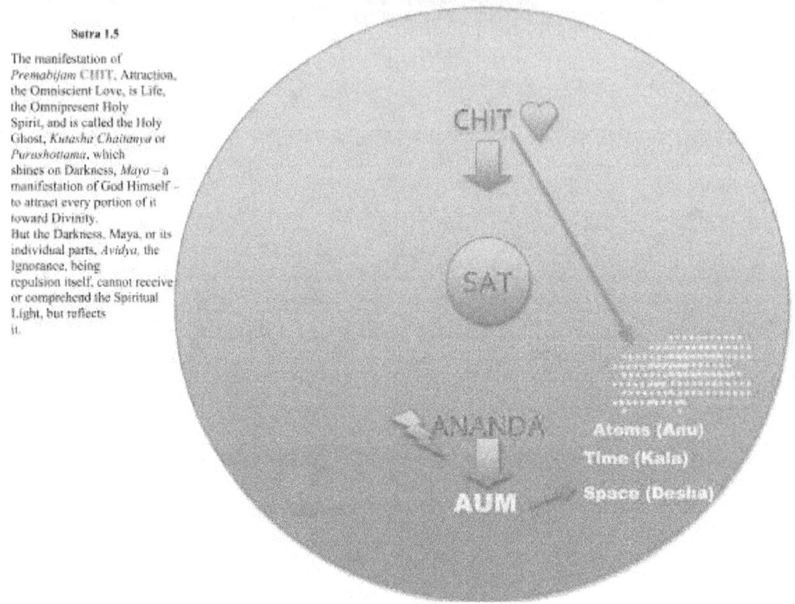

Sutra 1.5

The manifestation of Premabijam CHIT, Attraction, the Omniscient Love, is Life, the Omnipresent Holy Spirit, and is called the Holy Ghost, Kutastha Chaitanya or Purushottama, which shines on Darkness, Maya-a manifestation of God Himself - to attract every portion of it toward Divinity.

But the Darkness, Maya, or its individual parts, Avidya, the Ignorance, being repulsion itself, cannot receive or comprehend the Spiritual Light, but reflects it.

CHIT

SAT

ANANDA

AUM

Atoms (Anu)

Time (Kala)

Space (Desha)

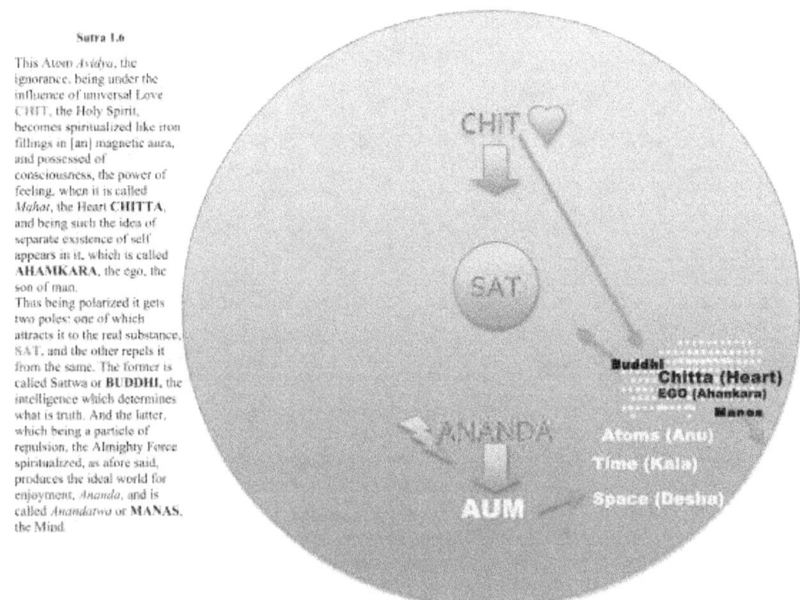

Sutra 1.6

This Atom Avidya, the ignorance, being under the influence of universal Love CHIT, the Holy Spirit, becomes spiritualized like iron fillings in [an] magnetic aura, and possessed of consciousness, the power of feeling, when it is called Mahat, the Heart CHITTA, and being such the idea of separate existence of self appears in it, which is called AHAMKARA, the ego, the son of man.

Thus being polarized it gets two poles: one of which attracts it to the real substance, SAT, and the other repels it from the same. The former is called Sattwa or BUDDHI, the intelligence which determines what is truth. And the latter, which being a particle of repulsion, the Almighty Force spiritualized, as aforesaid, produces the ideal world for enjoyment, Ananda, and is called Anandatwa or MANAS, the Mind.

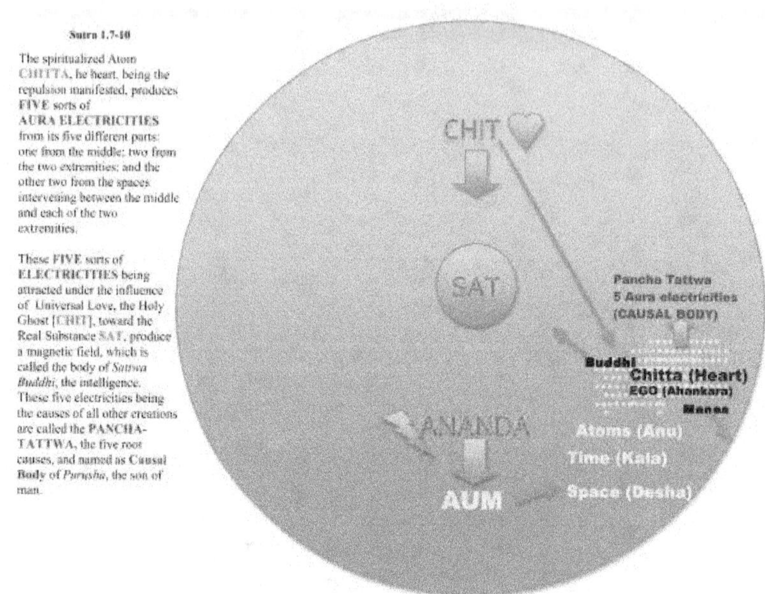

Sutra 1.7-10

The spiritualized Atom CHITTA, he heart, being the repulsion manifested, produces FIVE sorts of AURA ELECTRICITIES from its five different parts: one from the middle; two from the two extremities; and the other two from the spaces intervening between the middle and each of the two extremities.

These FIVE sorts of ELECTRICITIES being attracted under the influence of Universal Love, the Holy Ghost [CHIT], toward the Real Substance SAT, produce a magnetic field, which is called the body of Sattwa Buddhi, the intelligence.

These five electricities being the causes of all other creations are called the PANCHA- TATTWA, the five root causes, and named as Causal Body of Purusha, the son of man.

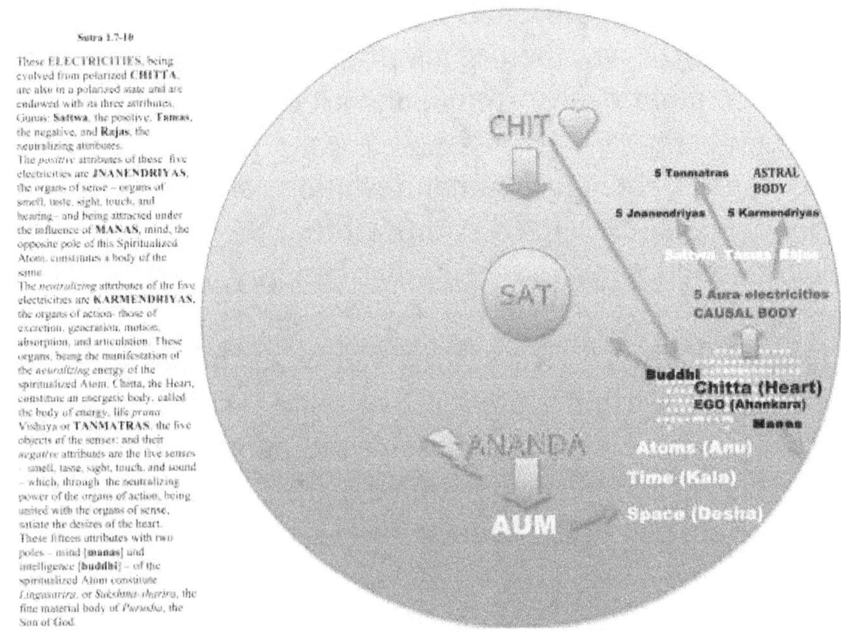

Sutra 1.7-10

These ELECTRICITIES, being evolved from polarized CHITTA, are also in a polarized state and are endowed with its three attributes, Gunas: Sattwa, the positive, Tamas, the negative, and Rajas, the neutralizing attributes.

The positive attributes of these five electricities are JNANENDRIYAS, the organs of sense-organs of smell, taste, sight, touch, and hearing- and being attracted under the influence of MANAS, mind, the opposite pole of this Spiritualized Atom, constitutes a body of the same.

The neutralizing attributes of the five electricities are KARMENDRIYAS, the organs of action- those of excretion, generation, motion, absorption, and articulation.

These organs, being the manifestation of the neutralizing energy of the spiritualized Atom, Chitta, the Heart, constitute an energetic body, called the body of energy, life prana.

Vishaya or TANMATRAS, the five objects of the senses; and their negative attributes are the five senses -smell, taste, sight, touch, and sound - which, through the neutralizing power of the organs of action, being united with the organs of sense, satiate the desires of the heart.

These fifteen attributes with two poles - mind (manas) and intelligence (buddhi) - of the spiritualized Atom constitute Linga Sarira, or Sukshma-sharira, the fine material body of Purusha, the Son of God.

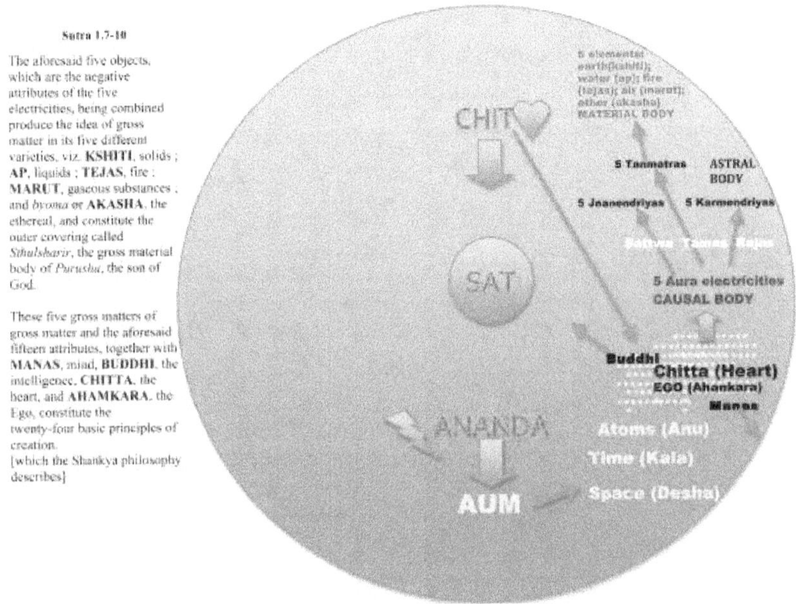

Sutra 1.7-10

The aforesaid five objects, which are the negative attributes of the five electricities, being combined produce the idea of gross matter in its five different varieties, viz. KSHITI, solids; AP, liquids; TEJAS, fire; MARUT, gaseous substances; and byoma or AKASHA, the ethereal, and constitute the outer covering called Sthulsharir, the gross material body of Purusha, the son of God.

These five gross matters of gross matter and the aforesaid fifteen attributes, together with MANAS, mind, BUDDHI, the intelligence, CHITTA, the heart, and AHAMKARA, the Ego, constitute the twenty-four basic principles of creation.
[which the Shankya philosophy describes]

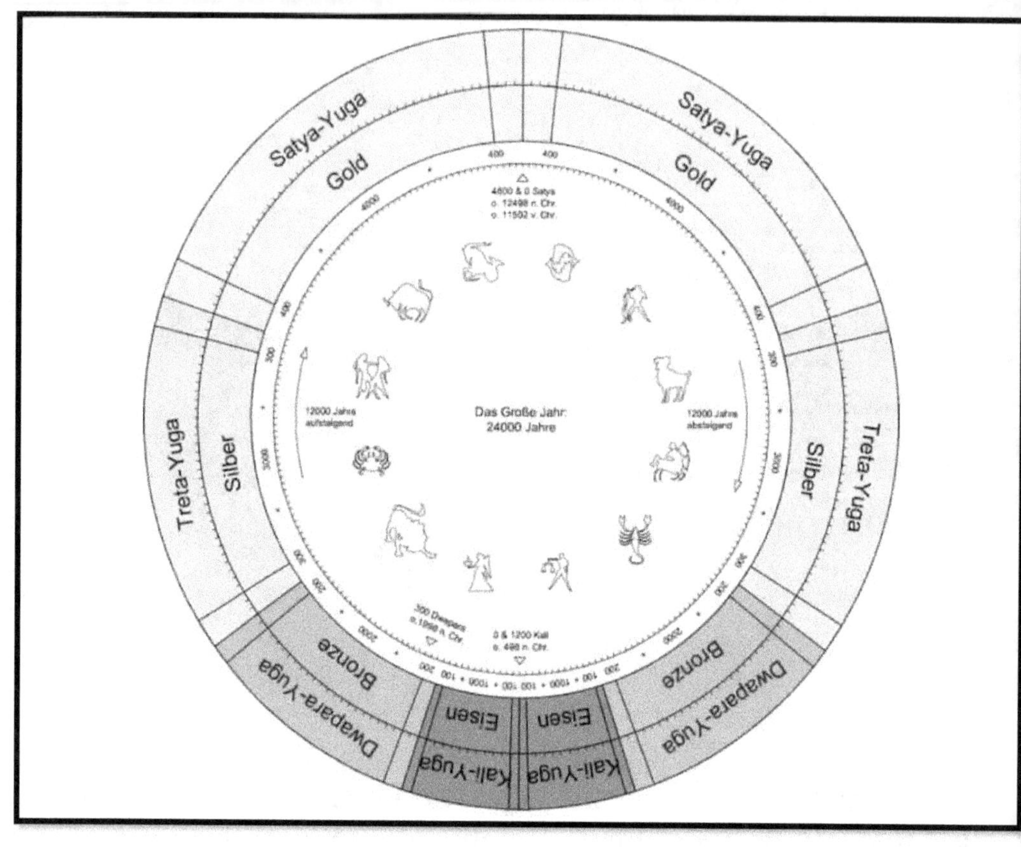

Satya-Yuga
Gold
Treta-Yuga
Silber
Bronze
Dwapara-Yuga
Eisen
Kali-Yuga
Das Große Jahr:
24000 Jahre
12000 Jahre
aufsteigend
12000 Jahre
absteigend
4800 & 0 Satya
o. 12498 n. Chr.
u. 11502 v. Chr.
300 Dwapara
o. 1698 n. Chr.
0 & 1200 Kali
o. 498 n. Chr.

Other Books are also available from **Swami Yoganandaji** at Amazon, Flipkart and Notion Press Store. You can open these links in your SmartPhone by Scanning them with Google Lens, then you can Buy, whatever Books your blessed self want.

Sr. No.	Name of the Books & Links thereof
1	371 Guidelines to Kriya Practitioners Amazon.in - http://bit.ly/44sKaSL Flipkart.com - https://goo.by/zFBQ2 Notion Press Store - https://goo.by/OESDa
2	Biography of Yogiraj Sri Sri Shyama Charan Lahiri Mahasaya Amazon.in - https://bit.ly/3YUr5I0 Flipkart.com - https://goo.by/VAbe3 Notion Press Store - https://goo.by/hRejg
3	Swami Yogananda's Super Advanced Course (Lessons 1 to 12) (1930 Original Edition) Amazon.in - https://bit.ly/3qRWxdo Flipkart.com - https://goo.by/cUCOu Notion Press Store - https://goo.by/1Jtuw

5	<u>Paramhansa Yogananda's - Metaphysical Meditations (1952 Original Edition)</u> Amazon.in - https://bit.ly/45S5oe5 Flipkart.com - https://goo.by/jmGi9 Notion Press Store - https://goo.by/W9v4G
6	<u>Original Teachings of Swami Yoganandaji Vol.-1 (Praeceptas Step 1 to 3, Lessons 1 to 77) :</u> Amazon.in - https://bit.ly/469kcFl Flipkart.com - https://goo.by/Kglr4 Notion Press Store - https://goo.by/GZBFV
7	<u>Original Teachings of Swami Yoganandaji Vol.-2 (Praeceptas Step 4 to 6, Lessons 79 to 152) :</u> Amazon.in - https://bit.ly/3YVsGx4 Flipkart.com - https://goo.by/nbann Notion Press Store - https://goo.by/6xqD2
8	<u>Atma Katha - The Authorized Story of Sri Sri Yukteshwarji's First Disciple - Shri Matital Mukhopadhyay</u> Notion Press Store - https://goo.by/wLJ9A

9	<u>Scientific Healing Affirmation (1925 Original Edition)</u> Amazon.in - https://bit.ly/3OWsUj8 Flipkart.com - https://goo.by/lwpG0 Notion Press Store - https://goo.by/oxNRF
10	<u>Songs of the Soul (1923 Original Edition)</u> Notion Press Store - https://goo.by/ZDUJW
11	<u>Stories of Mukunda - Early life of Paramahansa Yogananda (1958 Original Edition)</u> Amazon.in - https://bit.ly/3R1t4bz Flipkart.com - https://goo.by/4K4iR Notion Press Store - https://goo.by/Blg50
12	<u>The Cosmic Mother - One Aspect of God (1945 Original Edition)</u> Amazon.in - https://bit.ly/3R4HIif Flipkart.com - https://goo.by/1bYpO Notion Press Store - https://goo.by/ismPM

13	The Rubaaiyat of Omar Khayyam - A Spiritual Interpretation by Swami Yogananda (1937 Original Edition) Amazon.in - https://bit.ly/45r2JIi Flipkart.com - https://goo.by/Bsu4m Notion Press Store - https://goo.by/1Gt8F
14	The Science of Religion (1920 Original Edition) Amazon.in - https://bit.ly/3YYqQf5 Flipkart.com - https://goo.by/GEKVY Notion Press Store - https://goo.by/0hy9E
15	Whispers from Eternity (1929 Original Edition with Signature of Swami Yoganandaji) Notion Press Store - https://bit.ly/3Pi2KHV
16	Swami Yogananda's 5 Yogoda Lessons of 1925 Amazon.in - https://bit.ly/3syEj0W Flipkart.com - https://goo.by/81sUn Notion Press Store - https://goo.by/Eo2t1

17	**Paramhansa Yogananda's Chief Disciple Dr. Minott W. Lewis' Discourses (Volume-1)** Pothi.com - https://goo.by/L03xh
18	**Paramhansa Yogananda's Chief Disciple Dr. Minott W. Lewis' Discourses (Volume-2)** Pothi.com - https://goo.by/YnKD3
19	**Swami Yogananda's East-West Magazines (Vol.1 thru Vol.4)** Pothi.com - https://goo.by/ofDam
20	**Swami Yogananda's East-West Magazines (Vol.5 thru Vol.7)** Pothi.com - https://goo.by/uZRGg
21	**Swami Yogananda's East-West Magazines (Vol.8 thru Vol.9)** Pothi.com - https://goo.by/XxtGv
22	**Swami Yogananda's - Comparison of the Scriptures (1932 Original Edition)** Notion Press Store - https://bit.ly/3EkzsTW

23	The Original Bhagavad Gita - A Spiritual Interpretation by Swami Yogananda (1932 Original Edition) Amazon.in - https://bit.ly/3swnsMq Flipkart.com - https://goo.by/unmzC Notion Press Store - https://goo.by/zvcAw
24	**The Autobiography of a Yogi** **(Original & Unaltered, First Edition, 1946)** Amazon.in - https://bit.ly/3OZ8fe3 Flipkart.com - https://goo.by/inBmjE Notion Press Store - https://goo.by/wCFJVr
	# UPCOMING BOOKS AT AMAZON & FLIPKART :
25	The Psychological Chart by Swami Yogananda (1925 Original Edition)
26	The Original Second Coming of Christ - A Spiritual Interpretation by Swami Yogananda (1932 Original Edition)
27	Cook Your Food With Yogananda - Delicious Recipe Booklet (1935-1936 Original Edition)

28	String of Gems from Autobiography of a Yogi (From 1946 Original Edition)
29	Swami Yogananda's Super Cosmic Advance Course (1930 Original Edition)
30	12 Set of Yogoda Lessons by Swami Yogananda (1925 Original Edition)
31	Aumkar Gita by Lahiri Mahasaya
32	Swami Yogananda's East-West Magazines (From 1925 to 1952 in 7 Big Volumes)

1. Blank Page for your Blessedself's Personal Notes :-